Foreword

It came. We were in the path. How do we, individually and collectively, find encouragement from an avalanche of discouragement? How do we move from pandemic pandemonium to a positive post pandemic perspective? What can we find from the past to vault us forward?

Centuries ago, in the year 1509, the philosopher Desiderius Erasmus of Rotterdam spent a week abroad in London writing down his thoughts. He was visiting another established humanitarian scholar and friend. The intent of Erasmus was to entertain his host, Sir Thomas More. More was later raised to a martyrdom sainthood—sadly executed for opposing the marriage dissolution of King Henry VIII from Catherine of Aragon in 1535.

The fictional story that Erasmus wrote, *In Praise of Folly,* became a major satirical work still hoisted for its insight to the world he critiqued by exposing its blights upon humanity.[1] The Christian Scholar investigated the ironies and superstitions of mankind, especially the decisions foisted by a church—his church—that had become much too restrictive and imposing. He was considered among the greatest scholars of the Northern Renaissance. He wrote what was to become his most celebrated publication in only a week's time!

> *The book's purported narrator, the goddess Folly, proclaims herself to be the daughter of Youth and Wealth, nursed by Drunkenness and Ignorance. She is accompanied by such followers as Self-love, Pleasure, Flattery, and Sound Sleep.[2]*

The brilliant satire transcended the ages for its creative commentary. *In Praise of Folly* made it all the way to become one of my college era term papers. Erasmus, the religious philosopher was well ahead of his time. In a sense, *Post Pandemic Perspective* is intended for the parallel purpose advocated by Erasmus—a correction to humanity. The period of the pandemic appears as a time to readjust thought and look at ourselves differently. Fate is upon us.

With the need of the annotated research element, and because very few minds in any era could possibly match the intellect of the scholarly Erasmus, my offering of *Post Pandemic Perspective* was projected to take twice that time—two weeks. Even then, the sense was that fourteen days would be quite optimistic. But, then again, as the author, I did not need to constantly dip a quill into a jar of ink—and the pandemic stay-at-home order had already taken effect. I began to wonder, "How will we come out of this on the other end?" Surely, there should be more compelling other-side-of-midnight projections to anticipate as the new dawn approaches.

What qualifies me, or anyone, to assert what positives should follow a worldwide pandemic? Nothing. Should a work such as this be compiled by a government bureaucrat? A doctor? A philosopher? A psychologist? Maybe.

Personally, I claim no expertise in any matter other than being, like Erasmus, a humanitarian. I could be considered just quirky enough to write this short book based on my unwavering idealism. I have long espoused a view that we, as Americans, do some things by archaic and ineffective means when we have the tools to perform these functions much better. I have been asked (twice) to lecture at Harvard on my views because, I suppose, my views are a little futuristic and subject to political acrimony. You'll see in what follows that I advocate significant betterments of simplicity.

The pandemic gave us all a chance to reinspect "what is" and then gaze at "what could be." This effort is certainly a conversation starter in that direction. What is imperfect can seldom be made perfect. But those that believe like me that they can be made less imperfect will enjoy reading on.

In the midst of the COVID-19 pandemic, it became clear by the end of the third week in April 2020 that nearly everything we experienced as humans in strife would be re-inspected post-strife. We would emerge much differently than when we entered. The first serious indication may have been the travel ban on Chinese nationals entering the United States of January 31, 2020. Like a storm in the Atlantic bearing down on the East Coast, the indicators worsened. But unlike the storm, this malady would stay and hyper-multiply. Reported cases increased exponentially. Deaths followed. America was at an eerie standstill economically—and philosophically.

There were few smiles to return; and even less of life's greatest potion— laughter. People were expiring in alarming numbers, and the concurrent residual was that funerals were private with no loving friends or extended family to lament or to herald the life of the deceased. And the deceased died alone, without family at his or her side. It became an odd time, indeed.

With respect to Erasmus, the long-ago satirist, today there is not much that we can take away with any sentiment other than sorrow and regret. But we cannot succumb to the dark side of tragedy. We must move forward as a society and build our new world once again. Another literary figure, William Wordsworth had written in his *Ode: Intimations of Immortality*,

> *That though the radiance which was once so bright*
> *be now forever taken from my sight.*
> *Though nothing can bring back the hour*
> *of splendor in the grass, glory in the flower.*
> *We will grieve not, rather find*
> *strength in what remains behind.*[3]

The tomorrows we will enjoy again will be up to us to shape and author within purposeful considerations of what we all experienced during the dark era of the COVID-19 virus. Our culture changed while we were home recollecting, reconnecting, and re-inspecting our lives in the fervor of what would follow. Perhaps we will have found something about ourselves in those unusual times. We may have rediscovered a deep well of creativity in our collective mindset—to benefit the post-pandemic world we will rebuild together.

This work is dedicated to those we all miss, who died in the "Times of the Pandemic." May their souls rest in peace, and may we remember them always.

W. Thomas McQueeney

Post Pandemic Perspective

Positive Projections for the New Normal
in the Aftermath of COVID-19

W. Thomas McQueeney

Palmetto Publishing Group
Charleston, SC

Post Pandemic Perspective
Copyright © 2020 by W. Thomas McQueeney

All rights reserved

First Edition

Printed in the United States

ISBN-13: 978-1-64111-890-3
ISBN-10: 1-64111-890-3

Table of Contents

Historical Context

Let's explore what happened and has been happening in the after-impact of the COVID-19 pandemic's dispersion to every climate, country, and culture of our underprepared world.

The COVID-19 pandemic will forever be associated with the year 2020. COVID-19 is simply the coronavirus pandemic that began in 2019—but entered the world stage in January of 2020. The highly contagious virus began spreading in Wuhan, China. The Chinese government took few early precautions and, as a result, the pandemic spread outside of China quickly.

Though the authoritarian Chinese Communist government put a halt to domestic flights into and out of Wuhan, they did nothing to halt international flights. Those travelers brought the virus to the entire world. In airline traffic alone, the daily service of 2.7 million passengers on 44,000 flights across 29 million miles of airspace gave the virus instant portability.[4] No country was completely spared.

Under a microscope, the virus exhibits spiked columns, giving the disease a name—corona—as in the corrugated spikes of a crown.[5] Coronaviruses have been around to the point that they are numbered in a sequence.

The scientific consensus was initially that the virus began in the Chinese "wet markets" of Wuhan where it came from Chinese food sources—blamed on bats or pangolins. Later reports were that they did not sell bats, leaving the rare pangolin as the target source. A pangolin is scaly anteater (mammal) that is highly sought as a specialty meat in China and

Vietnam.[6] No one is quite certain if either of these Chinese delicacies transmitted a deadly virus to a wet market patron.

We know that the virus spread rapidly in Wuhan and as of March 31, 2020, they reported 2,535 deaths.[7] But other indications by estimate puts that figure much higher—as many as ten times the reported number. How do we know? China's rate of cremations to death has remained higher than 50% for many years, yet the number of orders for urns during the worst virus weeks indicated a much steeper death toll that what the government reported.

The mammal Pangolin. Photo Courtesy World Wildlife Organization.

Trucks dropped off roughly 2,500 urns on both Wednesday and Thursday local time to one of the eight local funeral homes, a driver told Chinese media outlet Caixin. The news site also published another photo showing 3,500 urns stacked inside the facility. The number of urns that arrived in that one funeral home was far greater than the city's official overall death COVID-19 toll.[8]

Sadly, the Chinese historically do not share the same distaste for death as we do in the Western world. Authoritative regimes rarely do. Just over the last hundred years, Mao Zedong and Josef Stalin ordered deaths that dwarfed those of the more well-known executioner Adolf Hitler.[9] The civil world that we've known has too many reminders of those that have no regard for lives lost—as the vigilance of terror cells continues.

The authoritative communist regime may have been loath to report the entire story. A further report charged that the virus may have come out of a Chinese laboratory. Still, the Chinese authorities remained unwilling to share detailed information. There may never be an accurate accounting of the source for the virus, nor the number of Chinese deaths.

What is accurate is that these corona-type viruses come from animals. Scientists tell us that the spike-shaped coronaviruses circulate in mammals and birds. Once the outbreak occurred, the Chinese government subverted information as one would expect to dodge culpability. They intentionally underreported the cases and the death toll. World politics became a part of the pandemic process.

> *The strategic negligence of China's leaders helped make the coronavirus pandemic possible – it has brought the world economy to the brink of collapse and it is filling hospitals and cemeteries all over the globe. It is widely accepted that the unregulated sale of wildlife at open wet markets – like the Wuhan wet market – was the original cause of humans contracting the novel coronavirus.*[10]

Are there nefarious forces at work? Was the outbreak an intentional act? If so, what is the purpose? Conspiracy theorists point to China's economic goals. Again, we may never know the truth. The virus changed everyone's life and livelihood.

Massive transboundary human damage had occurred because of the negligence of the Chinese government to shut down the previously specified unhealthy conditions outlined by the World Health Organization—with warnings recorded years earlier. The World Health Organization

(WHO) came under scrutiny, as well, for misleading early reports that appeared to protect Chinese claims. WHO is funded by most developed nations—the US being the lead support contributor. The $400 million funding by the United States was put on hold pending a full investigation.

Many westerners had never heard of Wuhan, a city with a metro population exceeding eight million. Wuhan is the 39th largest city worldwide—with more than twice the people of the Seattle metro population.[11] The wet markets there had been cited often.

China had been the source of other reckless health policies in the past twenty years.

> *In the years since China carried out its "reform and opening up" policies and its 2001 entry into the World Trade Organization, the 2002 SARS crisis, the 2008 milk production scandal, and the 2009 H1N1 crisis have beset China and countries around the world. The Chinese people might have preferred life-saving health and food safety regulations over infrastructure baubles, but the ruling Party's political stranglehold on society permits it to ignore or stifle the kinds of popular demands for reform that have produced dramatic, life-saving changes in the democratic world over the past century.*[12]

By April 2 of 2020, the morbid news worsened. The Chinese government had continued to turn a blind eye to reporting the full extent of what they knew. Catholic News Asia (UCANews) reported:

> *No corner of the world is untouched by this pandemic, no life unaffected. According to the World Health Organization, nearly a million people have been infected and more than 46,000 have died. By the time this is over, the global death toll is expected to be millions.*[13]

Map of China showing Wuhan in the Hubei Province.

The beginning and end to the COVID-19 pandemic has yet to be fully explored, attributed, or scientifically tracked. Those exercises will persist well after the last life is lost to the sudden world tragedy. As we ascertain more information, more areas of information expand. The final summation may take years.

History provides us with even more devastating battles of humanity versus the microbes we cannot readily see. The four pandemics that would be most familiar to many include the HIV or AIDS virus, the Spanish Flu of 1918-1920, and the two Bubonic Plagues.

The AIDS virus only recently peaked (2012) and has killed an estimated 36 million worldwide. The immensity of the death toll is all-the-more concerning as modern medicine had been most adaptive to most other new challenges. New treatments have not eliminated AIDS but have made it more manageable and not a "death sentence certain."

What was once the Spanish Flu (a misnomer, as it did not originate in Spain) became the 1918 flu pandemic at the close of the Great War (WWI). That malady, which likely had begun in the American Midwest,[14] may have accounted for as many as 50 million lives lost a century ago. Its impact lasted through late 1920. Many more lives were lost than those on the battlefield in this first five-continent war. As many as 675,000 Americans died from the 1918 Flu Pandemic—more than the 618,222 casualties from the American Civil War.[15]

The worst pandemic tragedies recorded across time were plagues. "The Black Death" was the Bubonic Plague of 1346-1353. Estimates of the death toll were as high as 200 million.[16] The plague was brought on by fleas living on rats.[17] The rats traveled on most ships. The devastation spread from Asia to Europe and Africa.

The first bubonic plague killed off half the population of Europe from 541 through 542. Constantinople (now Istanbul) lost 40% of its population. Other cities fared much worse. In all, 25 million died from what was called "The Plague of Justinian."[18]

With the exception of AIDS, these historical pandemics had very little defensive mechanisms. In essence, they ran their biological courses and completed their maximum damage. Vaccines had made their first appearance around the year 1000, but their effectiveness for specific diseases took much longer. Some diseases, smallpox in particular, were used as war weapons. Edward Jenner in 1796 developed a vaccine that became an effective immunity to smallpox.[19] It became widely available. Science moved humanity forward. Immunities and preventions followed for rabies, diphtheria, tetanus, mumps, polio, measles, rubella, and Hepatitis B. Indeed, as the Greek philosopher Plato advised, "Necessity is the mother of invention." COVID-19 would not escape this sentiment—though the expedition of its utilization would save many future lives. As the world watched, developmental time meant lives lost.

Edward Jenner. Rendering Courtesy Library of Medicine.

COVID-19's spread had made it to every country by April of 2020. The April 15, 2020 report from World Meters stated the immensity.

> *210 Countries and Territories around the world have reported a total of 2,017,810 confirmed cases of the coronavirus COVID-19 that originated from Wuhan, China, and a death toll of **128,041 deaths**.*[20]

The morbid result became the daily death toll, especially among those at risk—the aged, the infirm, and the very young. The families of those who died during the pandemic had the awful prospect of a small funeral with very limited attendance. Lives well lived were not honored as such. For some, a celebration of life was postponed.

There were secondary and tertiary impacts.

The world economy came to a standstill. Airlines, hotels, cruise ships, restaurants, shops, theaters, galleries, and entertainment venues came to a sudden halt. Sports teams had no place to gather or to perform worldwide. Manufacturers were not manufacturing. Builders were not building. Incomes shrunk. Governments overextended their treasuries by emergency means.

The stock market suffered. The Dow Jones average of nearly 29,000 fell to 20,000 in a matter of weeks. Drops of 2000 to 3000 points in a day rattled investors. The common belief was that the bull market would return…but when?

People, ostensibly, were at home. It was the safest place to remain to avoid the pandemic. They were at home in Minnesota and Mississippi; New Hampshire and Nevada. And they were at home in Switzerland, Argentina, and Uzbekistan. Only the "essential members of the workforce" were able to move about with great precaution. These were the selfless medical workers, food workers, and emergency responders. They did so at great personal risk.

We watched the news as the numbers rose in uncomfortable chart lines upward. We waited for the crest and the hopeful flattening to a recess. It wasn't about the chart. It was about lives lost.

It was unfortunate that some individuals, some politicians, and some governments politicized the tragedy. It was a time to not be political or cynical—but to be empirical and empathetic. It was a time to pull together.

There would be no doubt that this pandemic would bring about change on a worldwide basis. There would be cultural redirections. The experience had become too painful—in lost lives, lost jobs, lost incomes, and a stalled economy—to not ponder the future beyond the sickness.

Underneath that thick sod layer of misery could be seeds of benefit to bring forward.

Defining Essential Industries

A partial list of essential services allowed from the Johnston, PA, *Tribune-Democrat* gives a sense of the complications that law enforcement would encounter in their performance of keeping non-essential individuals at home.[21] These essential workers had the freedom of travel, along with grocery shoppers, postal workers, and all people retrieving prescription drugs. State-by-state, essential workforces of medical, government, business and industry were identified. A more complete list to include the subset of identified roles and occupations were established.

These included:

Healthcare/Medical
First Responders
Food and Agriculture
Energy
Water/Wastewater
Transportation
Public Works
Community Government
Critical Manufacturing,
Hazardous Materials
Financial Services
Chemical
Defense Industry
Military
Selected Commercial and Professional Services

Since these essential service individuals could not be readily identified when traveling to-and-fro, the recommendation of carrying proper industry identification was suggested. These identifiers could be as simple as a business card or a letter of identification from the "Essential Industry" employer. The sheer number of these essential workers in each community became compelling. How could these workers further prevent the spread within their necessary interactions?

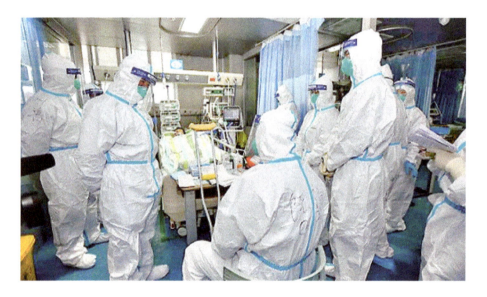

Medical teams suited up for the difficult pandemic.
Photo courtesy New England Complex Systems.

Much was lauded, deservedly, to the response of the medical profession—from the many doctors and nurses at risk who tended to the sick and the dying. Many additional hospital support staffers worked the hours of sacrifice at considerable personal risk. They were the most valiant heroes of the ordeal. There were also the first responders who worked long and arduous hours with often less personnel to manage a crisis previously unexperienced by an ever-adjusting society.

The medical industry component had to adjust in the heated of the caldron fires during the pandemic. As a pediatric neurosurgeon, Dr. Ramin

Eskandari cited, they were able to fully redesign their response in less than three weeks.

> *"The way I see it, never before in the history of medicine has there been a globally united effort to maintain standards of patient care to this degree. By that I mean that not a single health care organization could escape the threat of viral spread within their walls, and thus the world of telemedicine, video visits, and virtual health care was thrust into the spotlight of mainstream consumers. Up until this point, individual systems have argued internally about the costs, the logistics, the security of patient information, the reimbursement strategies and many more issues that the general population likely has no idea about. And yet, in the matter of six short weeks (four in some cases) universally across not just the United States but almost globally, these issues were solved to a point of mutual respect between hospital administration, providers, and insurance companies. If we were asked even three months prior, 'How long would it take?' the answer would likely have been in years—not months—and certainly not in weeks.*
>
> *I predict that our new normal will be a much more efficient, pleasant, and most importantly a patient-centric system of health care delivery. Yes, patients will still come see their doctors and health care providers, but they will do so when they are required, not because that's just the way we used to do things. That answer hopefully no longer crosses the lips of many old school medical systems and instead is replaced by 'How can we do it better?' And if you ask me as a patient, the answer is I want to be home and see my doctor via a web video link, review my problems, look at my imaging together, and when I really need to go in for a physical checkup, make it really count. And as a physician, I would rather see my patients in the comfort of my home on some days, have lunch with my*

family and finish the day knowing that those who I helped feel better, but are also so much happier not having had to drive hours and hours to see me. My ability to help is also no longer servant to a clinic schedule and waiting room full of people. My Online waiting room has only those who I am ready to see, and my patients are able to continue their lives while I see others until I am ready for them. Online platforms are getting more secure, more user friendly, and more accessible. The prognosis for the post pandemic health care delivery system looks very positive for those with an open mind and a finger on the pulse of technology."

The medical industry stood up and took on a monster. But there were many more behind-the-scenes heroes to cite. The agricultural industry responded mightily. The farms produced the nutritional foodstuffs needed to keep America energized and healthy. The truckers did as well. The commercial transportation industry was called upon to transport everything from ventilators to medicines to hand sanitizers. This was in addition to their upsurge in products ordered online by the sequestered and quarantined masses.

Bankers and the entire financial industry had new customers in a time-demand of governmental measures serviced through their drive-throughs. Small businesses, especially, were in need of the federal government's emergency funding to retain their employees and keep their doors open for the re-start of business as usual.

In essence, many non-essential workers continued to move about under varying claims of essentiality. The essential-ness of a person's intentions became more and more difficult to define. Yet there were pockets of "over-enforcement" of the restrictions—most notably $500 fines doled out in Mississippi for parishioners attending Easter services without leaving their automobiles.[22] Sometimes common sense lost out to common hysteria.

Emergency means were pressed into service. Two military hospital ships were dispatched—one to New York harbor, the other to Los Angeles. Field hospital tents went up, even onto New York's Central Park. The coronavirus death cases in "the city that never sleeps" reached into the 700s daily.

Yet, non-essential personnel made their way into Lowe's to buy hanging baskets and bird seed. Home and bored, they took chances that defied the law of large numbers. Somehow, too many felt that the mandate to stay home did not apply to them personally—just to all others that could keep them safe. This attitude proved to be detrimental to the efforts of the health officials and the governmental authorities to "flatten the bell curve" of the virus's spread.

The Center for Evidence Based Medicine did extensive research to ascertain the effectiveness of a 14-day quarantine.

> *Viruses don't travel, people do. So intuitively, we expect that imposing physical space barriers will work to eradicate infection. However, the effectiveness of quarantine during a viral outbreak relies on the timing and accuracy of the quarantine period, as well as the ability of individuals and health care providers to follow quarantine procedures. The current evidence-base is limited, and COVID-19 infection trends raise critical questions about implementation effectiveness.*[23]

As long as people changed the input to the equation, the equation would skewer the impact—and the result of needless deaths occurred. This indicated that people impaired the statistics by taking risks they should not have considered.

A better monitoring and reporting system will be developed in the future to curtail the risk-taking of individuals who hinder the suppression of viral spread. We all have been educated about predictable algorithms on multimedia charts. The flattening lines of reported cases across the country's landscape gave us the solace that the pandemic was winding down. We hoped to become one of the declining graphs. But people were still dying.

The New World of Social Distancing

Among the precepts of humanity, we can confidently assert that people are inherently social. We enjoy being around each other—even those we might view as introverts. We need each other. Yet an online trend of the last few decades may have inhibited some of our innate tendencies to associate.

The Millennials and their Generation X parents have been practicing a new form of social distancing for decades. The COVID-19 virus made the rest of us aware of the terminology.

Facebook, Twitter, Tic-Tok and Instagram rode in as the four horsemen of the digital apocalypse. If one could not spell "apocalypse," it would not be the end of the world! These popular online corridors made it possible for people who had never met previously to become "friends." Yet they may be faceless—or have faces that they once had years back. The exchanges that are typed and sent between parties are devoid of the human elements we have cherished for centuries—a smile, a wink, or a nod of approval. Emojis are a futile attempt to fill that void.

From Baby Boomers to Generation X to the Millennials, we have been stepping back. Social distancing has become evident in the implementation of social media, but also in the actuality of using the media as a substitute for in-person exchanges. Statistics bear the trend.

Traditional personal relationships are in decline. Previously, many of these relationships were relegated to couples who met in social settings like parties and bars—or the more promising atmosphere of a church. It became evident that other digital arrangements were being made for a fee on dating sites like eHarmony, Zoosk, Match, OurTime, and Christian Mingle. Romance went into its scientific era. Couples routinely meet online. Dating comes after the "match" is established. The pandemic will increase the online method of "meeting" potential mates. Will the post pandemic attitude of dating diminish even more?

The science of romance has positive feedback. Common interests and hobbies are explored. But marriages and birthrates continue to fall.

Dating couples have found a way to explore marriage potential through dating sites. Photo Courtesy Christian Singles.

Well before the COVID-19 pandemic, there was a growing concern in America about the decline of marriages and the resulting decline of children born within a traditional two-parent household. The Heritage Foundation brought this concern forward:

Families are the building blocks of civilization. They are personal relationships, but they greatly shape and serve the public good. Strong families make for strong communities. Conversely, family breakdown harms society as a whole. That's why America's declining marriage rate is a real problem.

While on the surface this might not seem like an issue that you and I need to care about, the decline in marriage has a significant impact on each and every one of us—from the amount of taxes we pay to the level of crime in our neighborhoods. How do we know?

Decades of statistics have shown that, on average, married couples have better physical health, more financial stability, and greater social mobility than unmarried people. Other studies show that the children of those couples are more likely to experience higher academic performance, emotional maturity, and financial stability than children who don't have both parents in the home.

The social and economic costs of family breakdown are paid by everyone.

Studies show divorce and unwed childbearing cost taxpayers over $110 billion each year. But the real victims are children. Children raised in single-parent homes are statistically more likely to abuse drugs and alcohol, exhibit poor social behaviors, and commit violent crimes. They're also more likely to drop out of school.

And when it comes to fighting poverty, there is no better weapon than marriage. In fact, marriage reduces the probability of child poverty by 80%.

So, what can and should be done?

When it comes to public policy, one-way government can help is by eliminating the marriage penalty. That's the part of the tax code where two people are taxed more if they're married than if they're single.

Second, government assistance programs should provide temporary help to families in need, not welfare that spans generations. For too long, these programs have encouraged the formation of single-parent families by taking the place of breadwinning fathers or mothers. But more family-friendly public policies like these are only part of the solution.

Civil society—including community organizations, schools, and places of religious worship—must do its part to make sure the next generation understands the hard facts about the benefits of marriage and the costs of broken families. Armed with that knowledge, people can make better choices.

Marriage remains America's strongest anti-poverty, anti-crime, pro-health institution. It's an undeniable fact that the best chances for financial success, emotional well-being, and good health for both parents and children happen when parents are married and families are intact.[24]

The decline in marriage rates has also impacted birth rates. The pause for a pandemic will only exacerbate this statistic. An excerpt from National Public Radio gives the overview.

The U.S. birthrate fell again in 2018, to 3,788,235 births — representing a 2% drop from 2017. It's the lowest number of births in 32 years, according to a new federal report. The numbers also sank the U.S. fertility rate to a record low. Not since 1986 has the U.S. seen so few babies born.[25]

Facebook did not do this alone. Societal norms had changed. People living alone nearly doubled in America over the last fifty years.[26] This exacerbated the misery for well-too-many in the pandemic.

Social distancing was the health officials' term that instructed a spacing of at least six feet. It was thought to be a proper distance to avoid the airborne virus in public settings. In the post-pandemic world, physical social connection could be on the rise.

Think of it as you would the 21st Amendment. In 1933, the 21st Amendment repealed the 18th Amendment of 1919. Americans had fourteen years of temperance—no legal alcohol. Like the repeal of the amendment, the "repeal" of social distancing directives will be happily accepted.

The pandemic sequestered people away from their grandparents, their best friends, their neighbors, and perhaps their romances. The sentiment was unpopular with nearly all. Humanity needs the warmth and care of others near. "When this is over, we'll have to get together," or "Let's meet for dinner." People want to change the social distancing dynamic in the way that they wanted to repeal alcoholic beverages as contraband. We might even expect a significant spike in marriage and birth rates.

Conversely, there are some that lament the enforced time of being with loved ones. They weren't that loved, after all. For a few, it was a time to readdress the commitment of a relationship.

What can be changed in romance—and marriage and birth rates—is part of what can be changed in society. The ability for a society to adapt to time saving and leisure-building models of work production will help. Government plays a vital role. They should find ways, by education and incentives, to curtail the tax and welfare benefits of single parent households. We know too many cohabitating couples, some with multiple children, who do not marry because a strong governmental disincentive helps them "game the system." The American taxpayer should rail against these unmerited government programs.

Social distancing has wide connotations. We've explored the digital trend, the impact of the marriage trend, and the physical virus trend. The terminology will remain in our lexicon—with each societal concept in its place and we in our place.

Governmental Responsiveness

It may be another hundred years before mankind faces another drastic pandemic. But there will be plenty of stockpiled ventilators. Warehouses will have them sanitized, sealed, and ready for action. There will be masks, too…and tons of bathroom tissue bought at a discount at Walmart from consumer returns. The government will be ready.

Congress in Session. Courtesy Library of Congress.

The quick answer to any microbial attack on humanity will always be the antidote—a vaccine or medication that repels the virus. Scientists are diligent in this regard. However, these viruses have adaptation abilities. It is imperative that science stays ahead of the mutations anticipated.

New manuals will come out of the experience. New laws will be passed. Enhanced responses will be necessary to minimize the loss of life.

Perhaps the major take-away of the COVID-19 tragedy has been the federal government's relative response speed in setting up programs to assist hospitals, industry, individuals, and small businesses. That sentiment is notwithstanding the political nature of politics! It did not come without regrettable dalliances for the pet projects of those holding the purse strings. However, as the virus grew and the death toll mounted, the seriousness seemed to expedite agreements between otherwise warring factions in Washington. But political posturing from all points seemed over-arching. The American public became keenly aware of the needless volleys in the face of devastation. Attrition of those who proved most ineffective will, no doubt, be shown for posterity in the election of November 3, 2020. Or at least, it will seem that way.

One key concern that came from the requirement of congress to act was that not all of the house members and senators could be there. By March 27 of 2020, four congressman and one senator (Rand Paul of Kentucky) tested positive for the pandemic virus.[27] It became obvious in Washington and state houses across that country that the risk of assembly became too great. There had been no previous protocol for the situation. Thus, the experience will generate new procedure to legislate and assist in a crisis. It may be that each state and the federal government will need to invoke an emergency plan of cooperation that allows absentee legislators to participate in government without the inherent risk associated with assembly.

This academic leap will require much study and a foolproof and verifiable electronic online signature authorized by law and invoked by a mayor, a council chair, a governor, or a president. As is usual with governmental agencies, this new protocol will be highly volatile and may take an inordinate time to become adopted.

The secured signature already exists. It is being used every day by people all across the country. It is the same security one would use from a cellphone to transfer funds from a savings account to a checking account.

Frank Abagnale, a security expert who spent his career with the FBI and wrote the true-story bestseller, *Catch Me If You Can*, warned that the antiquated system that government utilizes currently is a detriment to any program's effectiveness. Waste by fraud would ensue.

> *While there are several alternatives, one option currently available to the IRS is a site that already exists for validating Americans' identities and their banking details – Login.Gov. This is a public/private partnership headed by the Government Services Administration that is used by other Federal Agencies to provide simple and secure access to government services on-line. It ensures an applicant is a real person and that he or she is actually associated with that real identity.[28]*

Previous government payouts were highly susceptible to fraud. The programs that began to roll out by April of 2020 could be at great risk because the government's records have millions of incorrect addresses and many taxpayers who had deceased. Mr. Abagnale is a strong proponent of secured and verifiable current identities for all citizens.

The monstrous operational responsibility of paying out funds for in-dividuals, families, small businesses and corporate entities fell upon the Department of the Treasury. Once initial checks and electronic transfers were made, it became apparent that the funding was grossly underestimated.

> *The initial $349 billion pool for emergency loans for small businesses derailed by the coronavirus pandemic has run dry as Republicans and Democrats squabble over how to replen-ish the relief program. The Treasury Department and Small Business Administration (SBA) have tapped the entirety of funding allotted for the Paycheck Protection Program (PPP), which offers forgivable loans to small businesses intended to keep workers on the payroll and small firms from going under. "The SBA is currently unable to accept new applications for the Paycheck Protection Program based on available appro-priations funding. Similarly, we are unable to enroll new PPP lenders at this time," the SBA said.[29]*

Identifying ourselves has been a problem in the United States for many decades. It's true that we are a melting pot of ethnicities, cultures, and religion. But we don't really know exactly who we are and how many we are. Adversarial political parties want to define us in differing ways—those that are here because they are legal citizens and those that others want counted and extended all benefits even though they have not become legal citizens. One party calls them illegal aliens; the other undocumented immigrants. The semantics aside, they are the same in number, but we do not know what that number is. It is a source of conjecture.

> *Estimates of the number of undocumented immigrants living in the U.S. range from 10.5 million to 12 million, or approximately 3.2%–3.6% of the population.*[30]

Since 2020 rolled in as a census year mired amidst a pandemic, the ability to find an accurate count of all legal or even the "undocumented" American population may not have been available. Census results have a great bearing on elections and federal funding. With the additional pulse of a presidential election year, a pandemic became the most unwelcome "alien" of all.

By mid-April of 2020, there was a growing segment of population that clamored to re-open the schools, the restaurants, and the retailers. They wanted normalcy even though in some pockets of population the "crest" of the reported cases had not yet occurred. An underbelly of destructive social indicators—some pointed out—had overtaken the virus death toll. They cited drug addiction, alcoholism, suicide, and mental illness. The job losses and the lack of social interaction had taken a toll. The country was rushing toward a solution as the social distancing began to impact the reported cases. But there was a larger concern that the virus spread would re-emerge. Most scientists believed that the planned leveling and decline of the death numbers would spike once the mandatory stay-at-home orders were lifted.

On April 16 of 2020, President Donald Trump announced a three-phase plan to re-start the American economy that would initiate as the virus statistics showed a standardized trend of decreased cases. Some states, notably South Dakota, were already in a full pre-pandemic economic mode. Concurrent with the president's announcement, South Dakota reported 988 cases, 261 recoveries, and 6 deaths.

Center for Disease Control (CDC)
Photo courtesy CDC Atlanta

The driver of decisions that governors would make had much more to do with the actual trends of reported cases. In concert, science and medicine responded with effective treatment. The two avenues of resolving epidemics and pandemics are the same. Effective treatment breakthroughs must be developed as vaccines are constituted in laboratories for trials. Vaccines will become the element that eliminates the dreaded virus for generations to come, but until they arrive, we depend upon the therapies for those afflicted that are shared by experts across the world.

Fortunately, the United States benefits from the CDC—the Center for Disease Control headquartered in Atlanta. Throughout a crisis of disease, the Center for Disease Control has a massive obligation to inform us of symptoms, procedures, and reporting. They assist the medical industry with a high level of communication and effective treatment nuances. Their responsibilities do not necessarily stop at American citizens. They extend to threats of disease to American citizens, as well. For instance, the protocols we've witnessed via the media concerning cruise ships involve the CDC—even though passengers may be foreigners. The CDC has been fully engaged. Their mission benefits all.

> *CDC works 24/7 to protect America from health, safety and security threats, both foreign and in the U.S. Whether diseases start at home or abroad, are chronic or acute, curable or preventable, human error or deliberate attack, CDC fights disease and supports communities and citizens to do the same.*
>
> *CDC increases the health security of our nation. As the nation's health protection agency, CDC saves lives and protects people from health threats. To accomplish our mission, CDC conducts critical science and provides health information that protects our nation against expensive and dangerous health threats, and responds when these arise.*[31]

Government at every level has been stressed and tested. A rarity would be that anyone associated in these leadership roles emerge from scrutiny un-criticized—in most cases unfairly. In a crisis, the authority we have elected and emplaced is where we will look to lead. The best of the best will come forward.

Consumer Measures

Before the COVID-19 pandemic, many stay-at-home shoppers began ordering from convenience sources like Amazon Prime. There were no shipping charges and the product normally arrived the very next day.

In point of fact, the digital world changed many large industries. Amazon Prime became the largest retailer on the planet. Uber became the largest taxi service and Air BNB became the largest de facto hotelier. All were created and thrived online. Indeed, it was propitious that society had transitioned to the nuance of digital living prior to the outbreak.

But as COVID-19 digressed to change the habits of all, there became no need for many of the digital travel services. Travel came to a halt. It stands to reason that it was at the same time that the cost of crude oil fell. The price at the pump stayed low while no one had a place to go!

There were many other personal appearance casualties—nail salons, spas, barbershops, and beauty parlors. The secondary "run to the shelves" past bathroom tissue became hair dye. Sparkling silver roots were everywhere. Then there were barber clippers. There will be very few elegant and finely coiffured Facebook poses coming from the time of the pandemic.

An April 2 article from *Marketwatch* reported another concerning statistic. Alcohol sales had jumped 243% for the week ending on March 21. Pre-mixed cocktails led the way followed by beer and wine.[32] An optimist would report that homes had secured significant secondary virus protections that week. Alcohol does disinfect. Perhaps families were toasting the new Payroll Protection Plan or the CARES Act. These announced programs were met with universal welcome.

Tax-paying individuals were included in the massive emergency spending package. The CARES Act was charged with an enormous task—provide funds to individuals and families with some sense of immediacy. But there would be problems—millions of them. The disbursement became an unwieldy program of delivery remanded to the Department of the Treasury.

> *To make the payments, the IRS will use a master file taken from tax filings for 2019 and 2018. The CARES Act authorizes the IRS to send out between $1,200 and $2,000 to individuals, or $2,400 to couples filing joint tax returns. The actual amount is dependent on how much they earned. Additional payments are available for parents of children under 17.*[33]

> *This all looks good on paper, but the reality is that the information the IRS is using is incomplete. Its data don't account for the fact that in 2018 and 2019 there were 2.8m deaths in the US and 3.7m births. Further, every year about 2.4m American couples divorce. Without adjusting for these demographic dynamics, the IRS risks making payments to people who are dead, sending inaccurate amounts to those divorced, and completely failing to pay those with recently-born children.*[34]

The CARES Act would certainly miss many needy taxpayers and would require the Feds to find new ways to keep their massive files current. The Act would also eliminate perhaps millions of income-earning Americans who do not file taxes—legally and illegally. Then there are those who pounce upon these programs nefariously. Only time will tell the cost of fraud.

Small businesses seemed to have a more critical need so that employees could be retained. In the first week of April 2020 alone 6.6 unemployment claims were filed.[35] Unemployment would need to transition to re-employment to salvage a flagging economy.

Though these small businesses suffered, there were larger foundation businesses that were devastated like cruise lines, auto manufacturing, and airlines.

Cruise lines are a conundrum in a crisis. While the United States may be helpful to their unemployed US citizens, the ships themselves are registered elsewhere. Though many of the cruise line employees are US citizens and corporate offices like those for Carnival are located in Miami, Holland America in Seattle, the cruise corporations have long elected to enjoy tax benefits of foreign registry. Carnival Cruise Lines is registered in Panama.[36] Royal Caribbean is in the Bahamas, as is Norwegian Cruise Lines.[37] Though the federal government authorized a $25 billion assistance package to the U.S. airlines,[38] cruise ships are not U.S. registered and have no standing.

In general, consumerism had its pockets of sustainability, but had a forecast of doom in the front windshield. Without incomes, where would consumerism grow? The non-essential businesses and industries were temporarily dormant. Perhaps new entrepreneurial developments would emerge.

Shoppers at retails establishment.
Photo courtesy of Tripadvisor.

Much was done by some small businesses that mitigated losses by their own ingenuity. Restaurants began to handle take-out, delivery, and drive-through only. Car dealerships began to deliver cars to homes after working new deals online. Relators showed houses by allowing prospective purchasers showings without others at the home, including no realtor. There were abundant stories of virtual real estate closings. One reported a social distancing closing done on the tailgate of his pickup truck.

Adaptation became necessary. Future courses of business are not fully determined, but a safe bet is that much more preliminary services will be completed online by the ease of DocuSign and FedEx.

The Humor of it All

Though the great loss of life across all of humanity controlled every news account, headline story, and radio talk show, the seriousness was nonetheless sprinkled here and there with the confectionary of humor. The public willed it to be so. Among the greatest of tragedies, there has always been a tendency to humor ourselves through the pain.

Social media may have been the catalyst that had otherwise reasonable people scrambling to the local Publix to stockpile bathroom tissue. The run on this product made no sense. In hurricane prone areas, people routinely stockpile bottled water and batteries. But that makes sense. Hurricanes can devastate an area, leaving homes without electricity for weeks. Water, being a non-perishable item, always makes sense. And nobody carrying 24 trendy beers bragged that they had a case of Corona.

In the case of toilet tissue, it makes no sense. Psychologists may place this under the column of a reaction to the loss of personal control of a situation. What will happen? How long will it last? Peanut butter or canned tuna would make more sense than bathroom tissue. One would think there had been a previous run on Tabasco Sauce and chili peppers.

The early online pundits noted that their local supermarket was out of Clorox, bathroom tissue, and paper towels. The run on these items began immediately. Perhaps it was a conversation starter for people standing six feet apart. "What's the deal with the tissue?"

The doomsday preppers had their own agenda. The gun shops had their best sales ever. The common concern with this population segment was that once it got down to the last humans living in bomb-proof shelters, everyone would want their bathroom tissue. Ammunition ran out in the gun shops, as well. We're all waiting on the story of "the great pandemic tissue raid."

Common sense dictated that there would be other developments related to the stay at home crowds. Well, nobody was stopping by, not even the mothers-in-law. And there was plenty of extra time to enjoy indoor activities beyond Scrabble and Monopoly. That resulting baby boom should have an associative name. "Vision Babies" from the year 2020? Pandy-babes? By the mid-2030's they could be "Quaran Teens."

In 2018, there were 34 million single-person households in the United States.[39] Introvert clubs could form with little fanfare. It's the perfect time to charter clubs of one. But there would be other stymied relationship activity in married households. Insightful divorce lawyers might have considered hiring extra help during the mandatory stay-at-home stage. The requirement that spouses spend time with each other for weeks on end would surely crowd their lobbies.

Church Canceled Until Further Notice. Sin at Your Own risk!

In neighborhoods, the theme seemed to be new hanging baskets, manicured lawns, and re-organized garages. People were jogging, bicycling, and walking after the home-cooked evening meal. Indeed, people were learning how to cook. Delivery and take-out meals were for the desperate family members who found out that no one in the home had cooking skills. The pizza delivery establishments were buzzing. DoorDash and Uber Eats had new lives. All delivery services missed an opportunity to add a roll of complimentary bathroom tissue to the order. Sales would have rocketed!

Social distancing became a standard practice prompting some who longed for companionship to remark, "Social distancing...I'm used to it. I've been experiencing it for years. Nobody seems to want to get close."

The COVID-19 impact went further. It was the first time the customers coming into a bank wearing facemasks were welcomed. Some of us felt like God has sent us to our rooms, but not without supper. People spoke to others by phone without the excuse that they had to go. There were no get-off-the-phone excuses available.

Song parodies flourished. My Corona replaced *My Sharona* (The Knack, 1979). There were remote skits by sequestered comedians without the benefit of laugh tracks.

Memes became the new online fad.
Photo courtesy Parade Magazine.

Memes appeared. These were humorous videos, texts, or photos transmitted to the largest audience imaginable—the quarantined.

The subject of humor may not have been shared by all, but was, nonetheless, often needed in the face of the tragedy. Balancing the emotions could be considered therapy.

> *Comedians unsurprisingly tend to be the biggest boosters of comedy during a crisis. "I think that you can joke about anything, assuming that the point of view you're coming from is essentially good-natured," says comedian Eugene Mirman,* of the documentary "It Started As A Joke." *"I think that it's fine to joke about hard topics. People need humor to unwind and to release their anxieties." If things aren't done cruelly, "it doesn't mean that they can't essentially be crass or something."*[40]

Perhaps years beyond 2020 many will look back and assess the tragedy in lives ended, jobs lost, financial duress, and the fortitude to face the new post-pandemic era bravely. The humor would have transported many through much of the shock.

The Education Paradigm

The last few national elections have brought college tuition debt to the forefront as an issue of concern. Baby Boomers had very little debt compared to those who followed. College savings plans of the 1980s and 1990s could do little to keep up with the escalation of educational expenses. Young people looked to government for relief and politicians were quick to trade promises for votes.

The COVID-19 pandemic changed the American mindset. Though there had already been a growing industry of online college course and degree programs, the practice of online instruction had not been widespread. Once every college student had no choice but to continue online, parents and students realized the efficiency of learning from home in lieu of other extraneous expenses. These included food, fashion, entertainment, and lodging expenses. College costs were likely to decline in the adjustment. The coming semesters should bear out that evolution.

The larger traditional public universities will always attract the 18 to 22-year-olds with the accoutrements of academia. These are fraternities, sororities, and social events that include attending large televised sports venues. One cannot tailgate online! The traditional pull of winning one for old University College comes at a cost in dollars and time. Simultaneously, the proliferation of college sports by livestream and other media had already decimated the university's athletic department lifeblood—fan attendance.

As technology becomes more and more advanced, fan attendance continues to decline. How can universities beat out the 70-inch television, the air-conditioned house, comfy sofas, cold beers, line-free bathrooms and surround-sound stereos that fans watching at home have the luxury of enjoying? Oh, and most importantly, the WiFi.[41]

Die hard fans from yesteryear were having their tailgate parties in their dens and on their patios in lieu of driving 200 miles to pay for an expensive parking spot where everything, including the food on their portable grills, could be ruined by bad weather. Media access took the revenue from the athletic departments. They, in turn, had the university increase the student activities fees to make up for the shortage.

Homeschooling may become more and more evident post pandemic.
Photo courtesy PBS.

And then there was the poignant moment when people realized that college attendance was for educational purposes. Everything else was "the window dressing." Their sons were not flunking out because of frat party alcoholism. Their daughters were not leaving to deliver a one-night-stand new grandchild. Home was much safer and more controlled.

Video technology has arisen to heights unimagined in years past. Western Governors University is wholly online. From 2015 to 2018 their student population grew 72% to 121,437.[42] Southern New Hampshire University advertises extensively. They recorded 104,068 students in 2018, growing by 73% from 2015.[43] Both online colleges will grow significantly going forward.

There are other advantages to online education. Classroom size has very little bearing. A top lecturer may address two thousand students because there is no seating venue, nor is there an audio concern. Support documentation, illustrations, and lesson plans needed for that lecture may include video that can readily be attached as a file to the student. Student grading can be done by electronic means efficiently. One nuance of the online dynamic is that the student may advance at their personal pace by completing the chapters and lessons quantitatively. By example, each lesson plan would have a quiz that would prevent the next lesson's session without takes and retakes until the student scores 100%. In this way, there are no failures—just slower learners.

Higher education will be Post-COVID-19 enhanced by more students at less cost. And that amelioration will be overshadowed by the shock of the K12 Post C-19 shift.

School systems across the country stopped the buses by early March of 2020. Young children were sent home, regardless of their parent's ability to care for them. Single parent households were hit the hardest. The social distancing dynamic prevented much outside assistance. Household incomes were at high risk.

Parents became facilitators, if not de facto teachers. Propitiously, nearly every home had computers and WiFi as it was packaged with cellphone and television services. Online subscribers had already begun replacing newspaper delivery customers for the large press establishments everywhere. A computer was fast becoming a necessity as early as the late 1980s.

Eerily empty Johns Hopkins University campus in April 2020.
Photo courtesy smapse.com.

At home with children to serve a role once set upon the American prairies of the nineteenth century would certainly herald change. The world was not conditioned to revert to one-parent households and rampant homeschooling. New dynamics would surface. Older students—high schoolers in particular—did not need parental oversight as much as the lower school students. How could traditional Post-COVID-19 education change?

Homeschooling will make a comeback and perhaps evolve to "neighborhood online" where a proctor would conduct the scheduling and testing of kids that show up on bicycles. A cottage industry could develop—like Uber or Air BNB. Smaller student groups at younger ages could be "group homeschooled" in a F.R.O.G. or a den on a large screen TV over the fireplace. Education will change by the pandemic wake-up call. We can do it better, safer, and less-expensively.

Trillions of New Debt

The final tally of new debt tied to the COVID-19 pandemic bumped the previous total well past $24 trillion mark. From where will that massive paydown emerge? When?

Economists suggest that the necessary relief packages coming from government will have a future cost undefined. The most optimistic formula would be to recharge the Gross Domestic Product well past the debt level to a point where the annual surplus reduces the massive accumulated debt. But the pragmatists would cite the more realistic future for every taxpayer—higher taxes and reduced government spending. We'll be paying more for less services.

Continuing on a path of unpayable debt can breed discomfort in the US treasury bond market and spur rapid inflation. The level of debt that our government carries is dangerous. Those danger signals are concerning. Nearly 40% of the national debt is carried by foreign governments and foreign investors. Nearly 8% of the debt is used to pay interest. There is a negative impact on wages for workers as paychecks flatten. The debt can also limit the government's ability to invest in or support key global initiatives.

We have to re-examine the reasons for the debt and find solutions that lessen or eliminate them. The cost of interest payments (the aforementioned 8%) is relative to the strategy of the other 92%. Beyond finding new and higher revenue (taxes), we must address adjustments in healthcare costs for an aging population. Key Social Security qualifiers should be adjusted with a transitional approach. Our foreign aid packages will need intelligent and predictive analysis. Other reductions may come from known federal to state redundancies which should be changed or streamlined.

The advocacy of a flat tax or consumption tax could become a timely discussion. The amount of energy and time placed in the unproductive activity (assembling, filling out, and filing tax returns) begs for a better system. A consumption tax gives government an immediate and predictable account growth. And it eliminates waste.

There are so many special interests—read "lobbyists"—against the idea of a consumption tax that it makes it nearly impossible to introduce. There are banking and mortgage interest lobbyists, daycare industry, education gurus, and seemingly innumerable others. But the consumption tax idea should resurface post-pandemic. Why?

1. Unmanageable national debt.
2. Unequivocal fairness. Everybody pays.
3. Predictable treasury proceeds.
4. Dispensation of unproductive filing each year.
5. Simplicity of IRS operations.
6. Impervious to fraud. No sentences possible for "tax evasion."
7. No reason for offshore accounts or tax shelters.
8. An ability exists to phase in the program and protect the minimum income payers.
9. Lower government costs. Lower taxpayer filing expenses.
10. Peace of mind.

One cannot flip a switch between the arduous IRS system of beleaguered time, penalty, and duress. There would have to be a plan to deal with what is now and what it will become. It could be accomplished by way of a five-year transition program by adjusting 20% away from the old plan to the consumption plan each year. For instance, if the full consumption tax is targeted at 15%, then the first transition year would be 3% plus 80% on the former plan. The following year would dictate 6% consumption tax plus 60% of the old tax, etc. This would give the federal government ample time to adjust and eliminate expenses accordingly.

One critique of the consumption tax would be the obvious disregard for those making minimum wages that would not pay taxes under the old system, or youthful non-filers who purchase items. These could be set up as automatic refunds until their wages reach a threshold of taxable minimums.

Setting up this system would eventually uncomplicate the treasury's ability to fund all avenues of American life with ready funds collected daily.

While the new normal sets in for all of us, why not take the time to find better solutions and better methods to benefit all? In the end, making ameliorative changes becomes the mandate of the people—not the lobbyists or the elected elite.

Given the passion for reforms in a democracy, voters are inured with the ultimate power. Voters can demand betterments peacefully and progressively by adopting the causes that build our tomorrows with the promise of integrity, innovation, and ingenuity.

Printed sheets of Ben Franklin.
Photo Courtesy of US Treasury.

A second wave of people-promoted cures to the national debt should come from a demand to balance the national budget annually by an amendment to the US Constitution. A balanced budget amendment has been forwarded, but never approved. It can be done by calling for a

Constitutional Convention. A balanced budget amendment could have the obvious exceptions for war or national emergencies (COVID-19 being one). It would have to be passed by a super majority of the fifty states (67% or 34 states needed). Forty-two states have passed balanced budget amendments or have that legislation pending.[44] Twenty-eight states have already passed legislation for a balanced budget amendment. We're closer than we think.

Many other democratic countries have successfully amended their constitutions with caveats that make sense to balance their budgets. Those reasonable elements could be incorporated.

Below is a sensible synopsis to support this measure:

Most amendment proposals go further than requiring a balanced budget or budget surpluses. Some of the most frequent additional elements are:

- *A requirement that the President submit a balanced budget to the Congress;*
- *Provisions that allow some flexibility in times of war or economic recession provided that a supermajority (typically three-fifths) of the members of the Congress vote in favor of a waiver;*
- *A provision requiring a supermajority vote of both houses of Congress in order to raise the debt ceiling;*
- *A cap on total spending (as a percentage of gross domestic product or GDP) unless waived by a supermajority of both houses;*
- *A limit on the total level of revenues (as a percentage of GDP) unless waived by a supermajority of both houses;*
- *A provision to prevent the courts from enforcing the amendment through tax increases;*
- *A provision assigning the Congress the responsibility to enforce the amendment through legislation.[45]*

While some may dismiss this key financial topic to assist us in reducing debt, the table for a constitutional convention is nearly set.

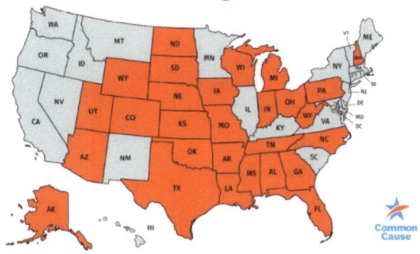

28 States with Article V Convention Applications for a Balanced Budget Amendment

Chart courtesy of Common Cause.

There are many concerns with passing the balanced budget amendment that relate to recessionary periods, interest fluctuations, and tax increases. Yet the overwhelming majority of economists see the move to balance the federal budget as a significant long-term benefit.[46]

There will be demands aplenty after the virus subsides. Every worker will demand a safe and hygienically secured working environment. Sanitizer products will be in restrooms and at desks. Workers will not come in with flu-like symptoms but may perform agreed upon online tasks from their homes. The American workplace will become the frontline of disease defense.

The avenue to building a better America will come from better Americans who do not accept the norm and demand betterment at every level.

Managing Religion

Easter of 2020 may have brought on the greatest shift of spiritual rein-spection in the history of America. Easter happened, but few were in church to be inspired by the most important day on the Christian cal-endar. Observance of religion was not limited to Christianity. Spiritual reinspection dominated the minds of those attendant to Judeo-Christian spheres. Attending churches and synagogues were put on hold without the traditional celebrations—the Christian Easter and the Jewish Passover. The Jewish population of the US is estimated at 4.2 million, or 1.8%.[47]

Though 73% of Americans identify as Christians, only 38% attend churches on Sundays.[48] Nonetheless, online megachurches have become the trend. These dynamic evangelical establishments capitalize on the niche of believers who have myriad diverse backgrounds. They aggregate at a second chance. They are the divorced, the born-again, the ex-commu-nicated, the shut-ins, and those perhaps bored by the presentation of their former traditional churches.

Some of these churches defy imagination. Their podcasts may reach many thousands instantaneously. Lakewood Church (Victoria and Joel Osteen) reaches 43,000 weekly "online attendees."[49] Life Church in Edmond Oklahoma has a weekly online base of 70,000.[50] The popular Rick Warren's Saddleback Church in Lake Forest, California boasts of over 25,000.[51] Seacoast Church in Mount Pleasant, South Carolina enticed 52,000 online worshippers for Easter 2020. Because of the online nature of these megachurches, anyone can join from anywhere. So many of these saw a significant spike in online attendance as a result of COVID-19.

Multi-site megachurches are on the rise, as well.

The Internet has changed traditional religion forever. Some recent statistics prove out the path of the future, well before we all had to stay home. A Captera church management report cited the trend.

The new dynamics of online worshipping is at hand. 54% of these techno-flocks tuned in to church online by video streaming. 55% of those that read the Bible do so via the Internet. The review reported that 85% of the mega-churches utilize Facebook to reach non-attendees.[52]

Trends seems to determine the future of personal and group spirituality. While Baby Boomers wondered, "How do we worship without a building," their grandchildren, the Millennials wondered, "Why do we need to dress up and leave home when we can 'Live Stream' services?"

What will be the impact of COVID-19 to church participation? Online offerings of video streaming will increase, especially to the Millennials. More will embrace technology as part of spirituality. The accessibility became more widespread and in the public consciousness because of COVID-19. It will also mean that participation will increase, though donations may suffer. Though giving online is simple and streamlined, it is not a function of public scrutiny. Conversely, a church pew has very few attendees who pass the collection basket without giving something even nominal. The lack of traditional church attendance will undoubtedly be felt in the collection plate. That loss alone may reduce the steepled landscape over the next decade.

Inside St. Patrick's Cathedral, New York.
Photo Courtesy Dioceses of New York

The amelioration will be that religious participation will grow. Online attendance means no nursery provisions for the little ones, no costs in time and fuel, no dress code, and no foul weather Sunday omissions. It also means that lesson plans can be viewed on other-than-Sundays and that those required to work on Sundays have an opportunity to view the service online at a more convenient time.

There will be exceptions. For instance, the Roman Catholic faith has no provision for video-streaming services because the in-person sacrament of Holy Communion is integral to that service. The communion hosts are handled by priests, deacons, and eucharistic ministers. The wine has been traditionally distributed sip by sip from challises. A new method of hygienic distribution would become an imperative.

Traditional US churches, in general, have suffered a decline in attendance over the decade from 2010 to 2020. The decline for weekly attendance by 2017 was down to 39% for Catholics.[53] Catholic population had also declined. The Protestant decline mirrored that of the Catholics. The only nuance to these traditional institutions had been the rise of evangelical (non-denominational) churches. That movement had a greater impact upon the decline of traditional Protestant churches.[54] Evangelical churches capitalized on many that had drifted from their traditional religions.

The evangelical outreach, especially the mega-church impact, had been active pre-COVID-19 in bringing their services into homes online. Among their most effective presentations had been the production of brilliantly showcased music pleasing to the attendee and the viewer alike. The transition of gospel music to the modern beats of youthful performers has established its own following.

It will be up to the traditional church leaders to find a way to showcase the church's online presentation as fresh, moving, and inspiring for those who cannot attend—or prefer to "get their religion online." In doing so, these church leaders must also manage a likely drop in tithing proceeds needed to fund the church's outreach.

A month into the universally realized pandemic, the concern of traditional tithing was realized. Pastors saw trends that the Millennials were less-than-generous givers,[55] and that the more generous Baby Boomers were aging out. In the crest of the pandemic, some churches reported as much as a 95% drop in congregational support.

To be sure, traditional religious venues had been in a malaise over the past five decades. The social revolution of the Vietnam era began the decline. The COVID-19 pandemic would shake up the reality of what had been working and not working during the pause when the flock prayed from their dens. The path forward would depend upon innovative thinking, new "business modeling," and a concerted effort to recapture the faithful by means not considered before the pandemical pause.

Religion in places that have attracted missionaries may change as well. By example, there are 37 sub-Saharan African countries where many traditional religions send their missionaries. The modern world has made it easier to find the unchurched in places like Africa, Asia, and South America. The sub-Saharan African nations alone have 444 million mobile subscribers.

It's a region where mobile technology is going through a major period of change, according to trade body the GSMA. More than 90 percent of the population were covered by 2G networks at the end of 2017, but more advanced networks are now beginning to take hold.[56]

How will the established missionary teams adapt to the restrictions of personal interaction in bringing the Word to those in need? Will the surge of technology assist or hinder their mission?

Religion will continue to hold a place in millions of lives. What form it takes and where it emanates will undergo a transition that the times of the COVID-19 will influence. What modifications occur for believers will, no doubt, be in the full faith of a loving God.

Office, Manufacturing & Commerce

Some traditional office businesses were forced to operate remotely. While this may have meant that the pandemic impact separated the contact of office-to-office workers, the more immediate reasoning was to subvert the office-to-public contact. The list of businesses utilizing the computer-phone-remote enterprise included law firms, insurance agencies, realtors, brokerage firms, and more. The enforced option opened minds to new ways of providing full services to customers and clients.

Lobbies were empty. People who had a reason to visit these smaller commercial and procedural components of society knew that the in-person visit became a non-starter. Innovative ways to do everything necessary by phone, FAX, online, or by video became the standard for weeks on end. The video meeting service Zoom was in vogue. DocuSign became more prevalent. Send, sign, and scan documents became a daily process—even for real estate closings. These processes had been around for several years but were underutilized. They were being performed by an office full of workers who could no longer gather because of the virus. So, why could they not be done from the family computer in the spare bedroom?

Insurance agencies worked remotely to service their clients.
Photo by author.

Office managers and agency heads did not want to shut down their services as they would likely exacerbate a loss of income that would be arriving regardless. Staying "virtually open" was as much a statement of resistance as it was a plan to decimate the economic loss. Staff members learned the ins and outs of promoting these small office businesses for their own edification. Everyone knew others whose jobs were lost for the foreseeable future.

Would there be a paradigm shift in office staffing? What would be the benefit? The downside? Some operational responsibilities could be performed remotely. If a preference of "home-staffing" became mutually beneficial, there could be a way to tap into part-time workers, especially stay-at-home parents who are assisting with pre-school or home-schooled children. Some hourly wage-earners could opt out of expensive small business insurance plans along with other costly benefits. Situations could be presented.

In many cases, remote staffing need not be specific to an area of each business enterprise. For instance, a part-time legal assistant could work for an office in Los Angeles while living in Omaha. These dynamics were rare, but already in evidence pre-COVID-19. The ability to "FaceTime" by cellular and computer technologies along with direct deposit paychecks make this a growth market of the future.

The nearly unprecedented wave of job losses had been somewhat mitigated by the emergency federal package that included the PPP—"Paycheck Protection Program." But jobs were lost, and people were struggling. Fortunately, the US economy had been thriving and unemployment was at or near all-time low percentages prior to the pandemic. In the post-COVID-19 restart, most of these positions would be rehired and an outlook of rapid GNP growth would result, lending a new positive to a bullish financial market.

Because of the new concern over proximity and contact with other workers and even equipment, a new wave of automation was bound to ensue. Machines would replace more hands and enhance manufacturing.

The International Federation of Robotics (IFR) reported the cost of robots has decreased and continues to decrease enabling wide adoption. South Korea has seven robots per 100 workers and every third robot installed is in China. A 2019 report by Oxford Economics predicted 12.5 million manufacturing jobs will be automated in China by 2030. In the aftermath of the pandemic, it could be many more.[57]

There are those that fear automation as a job-killer. However, automation paired with education will result in better and higher-paid careers. And there will be more jobs as automation accelerates production.

The new small office, the new manufacturing plant, and the new retail establishments would have a commonality of hand sanitizers. These key hygiene products had already been utilized in all medical centers and on cruise ships worldwide. They would now be available to assure the public in every venue.

The simple product would also make it as a staple of every home.

There were big winners from the pandemic. Stay-at-home shoppers found out more about Amazon and Walmart.

> *Nearly 1 million retail workers were furloughed in a single week recently, according to the Washington Post, and more than 250,000 stores have been shuttered, according to GlobalData Retail. Some analysts predict 15,000 retail stores will close permanently this year, which would mark a 60 percent increase from last year's record closures.[58] But not every retailer is suffering. For Walmart and Amazon, which already dominated a significant percentage of brick-and-mortar retail and online commerce in the US, respectively, the pandemic has provided an exponential boost to their already substantial businesses and power. Google searches for Amazon are at near-holiday-season levels; in-store sales at Walmart skyrocketed in March; and together both companies are hiring 250,000 new workers. Meanwhile, more and more people are switching to online shopping and grocery delivery and pickup — and they may not revert to their old habits when the pandemic ends.[59]*

It is a given that these giant retailers will own a larger piece of the retail market going forward. Both corporate entities, Walmart and Amazon, advertised for significant job additions during the crisis. Those unfamiliar with online shopping—mostly Baby Boomers—were left choosing it as an option unchallenged during the pandemic. In this way, the COVID-19 virus brought a larger market online for the stay-at-home shopper.

Just as Americans find more products to purchase online, the retail and delivery industry will adjust and flourish. The time savings could develop other positive advantages for the individuals, the family, and small businesses for the foreseeable future.

Financial Markets

We have learned to become effective in many areas of life while isolated. Those lessons will improve our lives and save us valuable time.

During the pandemic, banks routinely kept their drive-through lanes open for all transactions. Some would allow other financial services by appointment only. If there was any one industry beyond medical and first responders that was profoundly stressed, it was the financial industry.

The stock market seemed to be the emotional indicator of not only investors, but of all citizens. A bull market meant job security, steady pay, emerging markets, and more. The low fluctuations were much like witnessing the outgoing tide at the Bay of Fundy. Some days presented losses on the Dow Jones of nearly 2000 points. Imagine those that were watching the fluctuations of their 401K.

The stock market analysis had been that the Dow-Jones Industrial average had been near 29,000 just prior to the pandemic reaction. There remains a sense that those higher levels of market growth would return post-pandemic. But no one really knew how to define post-pandemic. A Harvard Study reported on April 15, 2020 that the social distancing dynamic could last into 2022 to avert overwhelming the health industry.[60]

The chart below shows the Dow Jones and its dramatic drop as the Coronavirus COVID-19 spread into countries around the globe.

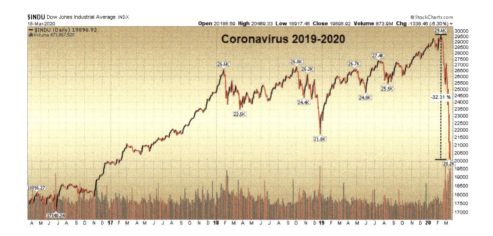

Chart courtesy of Marketwatch.com.

The 32% drop from February 2020 to mid-April was similar to the market drop of 33% at the height of the Spanish flu pandemic of a hundred years earlier.[61]

Historically, however, Wall Street's reaction to such epidemics and fast-moving diseases is often short-lived. According to Dow Jones Market Data, the S&P 500 posted a gain of 14.59% after the first occurrence of SARS back in 2002-03, based on the end of month performance for the index in April, 2003.[62]

The public following of the stock market for those who have no investment ties to it has seemed to be more of a bellwether concern. Some pay attention for indicator trends in other areas like auto sales or retail growth. The market had become the thermometer of the economy.

Courtesy of CBS Wall Street Images.

Forbes Magazine pointed out the expectations of investors that were waylaid by the pandemic.

> *At the start of the year, most investors expected the 11-year bull market to continue in 2020, only to be shockingly disabused of that notion by the spread of COVID-19. As a result, the Dow fell from record highs to bear-market territory in a matter of weeks. Investors need a way to price in risk, and as of April 2020, there are simply too many unknowns surrounding COVID-19 for investors to predict the economic impact, leading to fear and extreme volatility.*[63]

In the midst of all of the difficult news on stocks, the oil prices dropped significantly—a happy bit of news to the gas pump consumer, but another negative for those investing in the high finance of global markets.

Familial Interaction

In a way, the COVID-19 pandemic brought families together at a time that drifting apart was more likely. Baby Boomer families ate supper at the table together. They would often watch television in a den on one of three network channels. They went on vacation together, or to a picnic, or to a movie. These families were typically larger in the 1950s and 1960s. Cohesion was a given attribute. We lost much of that cohesion.

By authoritative requirement, families returned to their homes to find new traditions and new avenues to spend their new time together. We all have heard the warm stories of children learning the skill of piecing together complicated puzzles and learning the fun card games more prevalent with Baby Boomers. Some learned Chess, Scrabble, and Backgammon. Trivial Pursuit made a comeback. For those young entrepreneurs, Monopoly was always an option.

The most popular board game ever invented...Monopoly.
Photo courtesy stadiumtalk.com

America rediscovered family. It is the family unit that has traditionally served as the foundation of the American spirit, it's patriotism, its work ethic and it attitude of progress for the coming generations. Families could be found in every neighborhood walking in the evening, biking, fishing the lakes, taking out their pets, or simply sitting on the front porch watching other neighbors walk by. The greetings were genuine.

Though the close interaction was suppressed, the glad tidings were encouraged. A time when everyone was in a hurry had given way to a time when nobody had to rush. There began a new opportunity for exercise, prayer, music, and conversation. New projects were started. Old ones were finished.

The homeschooling activities and/or college online sessions turned each day into a schedule of accomplishment. Mothers, fathers and older siblings became proctors in the new responsibility of teaching at home. The daily responsibility became an integral part of the COVID-19 experience.

Families with previously diverted interests found new together time.
Photo Courtesy FOX News.

For so many, this familial time became a bonus unanticipated. The times were scary, the nightly broadcasts brought on horrible numbers of lives lost that even exceeded the Baby Boomer memories of the Vietnam War. Families were determined to make the best of the time and enjoy what would become memories of positive endurance and perseverance.

In all of the carnage from the time that the world stopped, it can be said that the biggest beneficiary had become the attentive re-composition of family and the re-establishment of community. Neighbors assisted neighbors. They passed at a distance on evening walks. Some shared home recipes or email humor. Others with sewing machines made masks. There were new quarantine-applied approaches like the "House Party" application. Neighbors employed "Zoom cocktail hours," and across the fence children's games.

The silliness of neighborhood restrictions during the pandemic were relaxed. Trash cans left out too long or a thick lawn that needed cutting became trivial matters unrelated to the re-engagement of kindness and generosity displayed by people in residential proximities. There were bigger matters to command everyone's attention.

Local, State, & Federal Governance

Government, at every level, had changed.

Local government responded by being both forceful and empathetic. They monitored the essential services so that the non-essential workers did not add to the algorithms of misery. Their ability to respond went beyond the preparedness it took for the shorter tragedies that they had trained to withstand—forest fires, earthquakes, hurricanes, and floods. A pandemic had not been in the manual. It would have to be re-written and those protocols established.

Town Council Meeting in Mount Pleasant, SC.
Photo courtesy Mount Pleasant Town Council.

State governments did not respond in unison. By April 3, 2020, there were still four states that had not issued a mandatory stay-at-home order.[64] The prevalent reasoning had been that the spread in these states was minimal and that the economic fallout exceeded the need to shut down all-but-essential business and industry.

Billionaire Bill Gates indicated the warning and solution.

"We're entering into a tough period," he said. "If we do it right, we'll only have to do it once for six to 10 weeks, but it has to be the whole country."[65]

What did we learn? In essence, the power to "make the call" on a pandemic shutdown rests with the governor of each state. There is no federal authority to usurp the authority of each state's governor. Thus, there are inconsistencies in each state's methodology. Some states banned out-of-state travel, while others allowed it. Pandemic-stricken New York State could therefore export the virus by allowing its citizens to travel to other states. States receiving these travelers outnumbered those that banned them. In addition, there were legalities to consider. Could a state actually ban visitors from other states? Could a state disallow its citizens their rights to leave? Under the extreme concerns of spreading the COVID-19 virus the protection of citizens everywhere depended upon the disciplines of the individuals well beyond the jurisdiction of each state's orders.

Another element of repressed activity came forward. The year 2020, as a presidential election year also carried the trail of many senate and all congressional elections. Candidates were stymied. There were no debates. Even the state and local elections were banished to the back pages. While nothing could be done about those circumstances, the whole idea of how we, as a country, conduct elections had an overdue public inspection. What would have been the issue had a national election been in order during times of a nationally mandated shutdown? In a sense, weather has long played a role in national elections.

It takes physically hardy voters to stand in line during a cold snap—or even snow—in northern climates. How does rain play a role in local, state, and national elections? Do the elderly "snowbirds" of Miami dare to vote in high humidity as lines form in Miami Dade and Broward Counties?

Voting generally takes place from 7:00 a.m. to 7:00 p.m. in each time zone. But there remain some workers, with travel, that cannot fit the voting activity into their plans. There are some that travel too far from farms. There are others that depend on voting absentee ballots—ballots that are often subject to fraud.

> *Absentee ballot vote fraud occurs when an individual commits electoral fraud via absentee or mail-in ballot. Examples include attempting to vote more than once, attempting to vote using the name of another person, and attempting to vote while being knowingly ineligible to do so.*[66]

Importantly, the major political minds and party pundits do not want everybody to vote. They prefer that voting should be an effort and sometimes a hardship. By shear numbers, one party may want to suppress voting in an area or county, while another wants to enhance the voting numbers. They read surveys to understand the benefit of high or low turnout.

The post-pandemic question that should arise, given the predisposition of avoiding gatherings, is why have we not progressed to electronic voting at all levels of government? The standard answers in the past have been rampant voter fraud, intimidation, too many uninformed voter ballots, and various other yesteryear concerns like graveyard names and duplications. In actuality, electronic online voting is the most reliable method ever. Heretofore, the absolute authentication technology was not available. It has arrived. It can be done.

Not only would it save the work of poll worker, election administrative personnel, and the closing of schools and other institutions—it would save time, fuel, and money. The United Kingdom, Switzerland, and Estonia already use this system.[67] Clear thinking citizens will demand it in the United States. There are no hanging chads, no paper ballots, no voter malfunctioning machines, and no recounts necessary. The results are instantaneous. The system would eliminate the worst enemy of this long-standing American activity—rampant fraud.

Types of voter fraud include intimidation, vote buying, mis-information, misleading / confusing ballot papers, ballot stuffing, incorrect recording of votes, misuses of proxy votes, destruction / invalidation of ballots, and tampering with electronic voting machines.[68]

Our elections should be pristine and unassailable at every level. We can easily eliminate the need for voter ID laws. The same recognition technology that allows someone to have simple items such as a social security card, a passport, a driver's license, a credit card, a checking account, food stamps, or any other forms related to everyday living as an American citizen would identify that person as a valid voter and certify that individual's valid vote from any number of secure electronic devices owned or utilized in the absence of ownership. It can be done. Our technology has reached that level. In this circumstance a person can decide to vote or not vote. But the identifying markers would verify the voter as a qualified eligible citizen of the country of proper age and registration. And that citizen could only vote once.

The post-pandemic sense of moving the country forward will spur a groundswell of Americans looking for better ways of more efficiency with less waste and fraud. Voter laws will change in every sector of politics.

For parallel reasons, the voters will engage in the way our country re-elects career politicians endlessly. Incumbency will be questioned—again for its excesses. In 1994 a political "sea change" developed around the idea of term limitations for federal candidates. Society will readdress this idea post-pandemic. Not-withstanding party politics, the public was sickened to see add on measures delaying an emergency funding package when people were dying, jobs were lost, and much of the population was panicked. It spoke to the games that career politicians indulge at every turn. The lobbyist impact upon career politicians had become a grave concern over the past few decades. The idea that someone should reach a senior status and spend a large segment of their time fundraising for the next election had become troubling. Congressmen especially, with two-year terms, had become the soft targets of political action committees and the lobbyists.

Understanding the dynamics, the 1994 election recommended self-imposed term limits—six years in the US House, and twelve in the US Senate. The idea worked in terms of electing new faces, but it did not codify the sentiment into law.

New Hygienic Protocols

A proper way to publicly sneeze had never been standardized until COVID-19. Touching one's face, especially the eyes or nose, became a consciously diligent warning. We didn't realize we were doing it, and then it became a matter of life and death. Sanitizing door handles and shopping cart grips became the standard of public hygiene. We became more aware of lingering microscopic germs that could kill.

We found that we could be carriers, though we had no symptoms. Indeed, the warning of public interaction had us sequestered and exhibiting a selfless neighbor-to-neighbor concern.

Shaking hands? Embracing? A kiss to the cheek? No. No. No. All manners of touching had to cease for an extended period until the deadly virus crested, flattened, and disappeared. Even bumping elbows—as was initially suggested—placed those participants inside of the six-foot barrier. A distanced, "How are you?" would have to suffice. Even the elbow-to-elbow greeting was abolished early.

An illustration of the expulsion of harmful bacteria in a sneeze.
Photo courtesy The Verge.

The public consciousness changed overnight. People carried hand sanitizer, handkerchiefs and Kleenex. We wiped down metal door handles, cooking surfaces, and even the hot and cold handles in washrooms.

Restaurants and theaters will reopen, but there will be a sense of a new lower capacity allowed. Tables will be further apart. Theater seats will be roped off. We will have to become accustomed to tape on floors to distance checkout lines and bank teller queues. See-through plastic barriers will become a universal standard.

Among the most difficult adjustments that may be required will be the procedures of pediatricians and dental hygienists. There will be many others. Everyone will feel the change in the new hygienic protocols.

We became more aware that we touch our faces more than ninety times daily. This practice promoted the virus to body receptors activity. It would become increasing difficult to curtail this nearly automatic response.

Restaurants would likely begin to supply hand sanitizers at every table. It may even become normal to see multiple people daily wearing surgical style masks. People will be quick to point out an unsafe practice to others like sneezing into the air, or into one's own hand.

A Reset Button:
Entertainment and Sports

The sports world—professional and college—have been financial markets within themselves. But everything changed when all of the NCAA spring sports put their schedules on hold. The pause turned into a cancellation. The cost to the NCAA and to those colleges who would likely have been selected to the Men's and Women's Basketball tournament was substantial. The member schools' projection of income was $600 million.[69] The NCAA voted to allow a $225 million payment in lieu of the tournament revenue, reducing the total college athletics department losses to $375 million.[70]

The National Basketball Association, Major League Baseball, and the National Hockey League followed. The NBA's initial plan of playing out the schedule for television in front of empty arena seats was dashed when Utah Jazz center Rudy Gobert tested positive for the COVID-19 virus.[71] Their thirty-day pause turned into a full cancellation of the season. The NBA projects a financial loss approaching $1 billion.[72] The National Hockey League losses were determined to be less.

The Professional Golf Association, at first planned to finish the Players Championship tournament in Ponte Vedra, Florida, without fans. It was an eerie concept to contemplate. The commissioner, Jay Monahan, relented within hours and cancelled the tournament. Even The Masters was postponed to mid-November of 2020.[73] The LPGA encountered similar cancellations and postponements.

Major League Baseball's season did not start at the first of April as is customary. The thirty major league teams left spring training sites in

Arizona and Florida without completing their workouts and fine-tuning for the long season. The revenue losses for spring training alone are compelling. Estimates of up to a $47 million[74] loss per team in Florida give a sense of what these showcases mean to communities.

Soccer fans around the world may be in denial. There are no bets being made at the Kentucky Derby. Rugby, synchronized swimming, and Womens' Tennis are on hold. There is no Pro Bowling Tour or NASCAR. Both the participation side of sports and the enjoyment of following your favorite players and teams have hit the pause button indeterminately. The stadiums are empty. The tracks are barren. The courts are stark and austere.

Horseracing fans may never get this close again.
Photo courtesy CNN.

Though viruses will eventually develop antidotes, there is no antidote for the revenue losses in the sporting world. The club owners cannot make up the revenue by ticket sale increases or reworking television contracts. Those expenses were already at premium prices. And then there was the prospect of reduced fan attendance since society had been stung by the proximity of others in the face of a global pandemic.

The entertainment industry took a massive loss, as well. From local symphonies to legendary rock bands, the lack of gatherings decimated revenues. Plays, art galleries, and county fairs were washed out as if inundated by the floodwaters of a broken dam.

According to *The Hollywood Reporter*, as many as 120,000 crew members lost their jobs because of the COVID-19 pandemic.[75] The New York Times reported the industry insight.

> *The red carpets are rolled up in storage, the A-listers holed up in mansions, multiplex doors are closed. For now, at least, the coronavirus has shut down much of Hollywood. And for the entertainment industry's many one-gig-at-a-time staff and freelance workers — a quarter-million people in Los Angeles County alone — it's an economic disaster. There's the hair stylist who can't do his job due to social distancing, the TV producer whose feature film premiere drew only a few dozen audience members days before theaters closed, and the event producer who fears losing her family home.[76]*

There was nothing essential about being entertained by the performing arts or viewing current athletic competition. As a nation, many of us were at home watching old movies, travel shows, and old clips of past sporting events. Knowing the surprise ending or the competitive outcome may have diminished the viewing somewhat, but it was all we had at the time we had it.

Fans at a live concert.
Photo courtesy of Loudwire.

Where will these massive iconic industries go after the reality of the pandemic subsides?

By conjecture, they are doomed to resume. That is, they cannot recapture what is lost. They have to simply move ahead in some fashion—in hopes that their audience reconstitutes and joins them forward. There may be a significant delay before people get used to being with a massive amount of other people again. The introduction of a preventative COVID-19 vaccine will assure crowds—whether they be assembled for outdoor concerts, college football, or mega-churches. The vaccine is the key. A delay of the vaccine will not bode well for iconic sports, the entertainment industry, or the classical arts.

The big-crowd ticket revenue will suffer in the immediate future. Until there is a vaccine—which has empirical trials and excruciating time sensitivity to the large gathering industries—both sports and entertainment venues will likely not return with the immediacy of other economic pillars. It is because COVID-19 treatment is a temporary substitute for the ultimate solution—vaccination. Until there is a vaccination, crowds will be loath to gather. Tourism will dwindle, as well. The vaccine is the divider between a prosperous large gathering return venue and the more likely de-emphasis of rock band concerts, NASCAR, and mega food and wine festivals.

In terms of sports and entertainment, gatherings will change for the foreseeable future. We may see several years before crowds return to pre-2020 levels.

Peripheral World Awareness

There has been much time to contemplate the "bucket list" of what is left. Whether each of us adjusts or not, the world has changed. Indeed, it was a world response that took place. It was a world that craves the fast forward button but is stuck on the pause. The world had its own pockets of travel ban restrictions. And the world will have to adapt to the "new normal" and move to the future.

Travel within our world will be the first level of change. Airports that had already adapted restrictive protocol since the terrorist attacks of September 11, 2001, will screen for other indicators than weapons. They will look at health and well-being. Those entering countries with elevated temperature ranges may be detained for medical evaluations and testing. Countries will have no choice but to protect their citizens—not only from questionable foreigners—but from concerning health indicators of foreigners.

Will air travel take larger precautions aboard their jetliners. Will their forced air systems purify potential microbes at 99.99% like common sanitizer gels? Will the public re-embrace air travel? Will we try new foods in the faraway lands we visit? Will we find our way back to 2019?

The multiple and layered travel bans have had an impact upon the re-establishment of national borders. Will the COVID-19 experience speed up the intention of building a wall on the US southern border? Will there be a sense of accounting for illegal aliens despite the vitriol attached to this subject in the recent past?

China. The culprit. They may become ostracized even by their closest allies—the Russians. On April 13, 2020, Russia experienced its largest daily increase of cases at 2,558.[77] Two days later an outbreak was reported on their border with China. By April 18, new Russian reported cases reached 4,785 in one day.[78] Total Russian cases approached 40,000 with nearly half in Moscow. It remains to be seen how the Russo-Chinese relationship will not degenerate, given the Chinese culpability.

In the area of reparations, attention to China's lending policies were being focused upon. Among nations, China is the leading worldwide lender.

In total, the Chinese state and its subsidiaries have lent about $1.5 trillion in direct loans and trade credits to more than 150 countries around the globe. This has turned China into the world's largest official creditor — surpassing traditional, official lenders such as the World Bank, the IMF, or all OECD creditor governments combined.[79]

At least a dozen countries owe China 20% or more of their GNP.[80] These countries—Djibouti, Tonga, Maldives, the Republic of the Congo, Kyrgyzstan, Cambodia, Niger, Laos, Zambia, Samoa, Vanuatu, and Mongolia[81]—have intense concerns of what the global community may do in the aftermath of China's reckless negligence.

Our world has learned to become adaptive.

By example, the military has codified important protocols. At the end of an insurgency campaign every colonel, admiral, or general would post a report of their respective commands that outlines the actions, results, and insights. What could be done better?

This protocol bodes well for doctors, police, and government officials. In the heat of the battle, not all things go right. But all intentions of procedures are set to secure a positive outcome. Along the way there will always be many critics. It's the way of the world.

The peripheral of countries who have found new ways to share vital information bodes well going forward. This global cooperation during the throes of the pandemic, with the damnable exception of the Chinese Communist regime, have paved the way for new dialogue between nations. The world's vitality and health are integral to the world economy.

Responsible governments have shared statistics, trials, and insights through-out the crisis.

Wuhan has a population of 8.3 million.
Photo by axios.com.

Pandemics do not occur very often. The "manual" on Coronavirus COVID-19 is yet to be written. There will be corrective measures, new scientific results, and a plan for storing pertinent non-perishable supplies. And posterity will dictate which actions taken by mayors, governors and even the president were most timely and appropriate—and most foolhardy. It is difficult to measure or grade those performances without "being in their shoes."

It is truly unfortunate for all office holders and those vying for politi-cal office that the COVID-19 pandemic occurred in an election year. The excitable press, the political party chairs, and the personal agenda large donors would all engage in the odd circumstances to elect key voices.

Will we trust other governments to hold humanitarian concepts ahead of political benefit going forward? The United States, after all, is the most economically advantaged country in the world. We are the most produc-tive country. The jealousies of others have manifested over the decades.

There have been threats from the North Koreans. The Russians have been nearly "blood enemies" for a century. The Chinese have certainly played the most recent Tarot card of distrust and misdirection. There are others. Despite our annual aid packages to provide medicine and sustenance to those in need, prickly dictators emerge to control governments. Our dedication to others is often misplaced as aid rarely filters to their citizens' need. Economic support to many of these third world nations must be reevaluated.

And then there are those that find blame from within. Despite enormous and tireless response of all levels of government, critics seem to take everything to a political level to lambast leadership here, there, and everywhere. If mistakes are made, they are summarily corrected. No one has other interests than that of preserving humanity at a time when people die from something invisible. But the critics seem to see a chance to politicize death as an agenda that suits their personal ideologies from both sides of the major political spectrum. Let's hope that voters see the difference between the sincerity of preservative effort and the rancor of extremists.

There is much to learn, much to lament, and much more to plan ahead.

The Predictive Analysis

As a nation we find ourselves seeking corrective measures to keep our families, our businesses, and our economy safe. But we must look beyond to the lessons that this devastation taught us about the world around us. How can we improve our society, and thus, our lives? There may be more than a dozen concepts to consider, but the following "take-aways" should serve as a basis to open the conversations:

1. The financial impact of COVID-19 will last for decades in terms of inflation, higher taxes, and lending rates. A groundswell people-generated definitive movement to a federal consumption tax should follow.

2. A national crisis of emergency will require temporary impairments to constitutional precepts, especially the first amendment. There has to be a protocol of authority that will allow this in the future for the benefit of all.

3. New ways to congregate for meetings will become part of the culture—most notably enhanced by online tools like Zoom. These innovations can save travel, time, and expense.

4. Governmental crisis development will require anticipatory planning and emergency supplies that can be transported from Federal centers. Professional and effective response to national emergencies will benefit mankind by their added ability to expedite.

5. Hygienic education and improvements to procedures and public protocol will be implemented. These precepts should be practiced and taught at home and in schools.

6. Education will enter a new age of controlled cost management to include the rapid growth of online high school and college curricula. Colleges will adopt "online options" in order to sustain their viability.

7. Online voting will become much debated and highly scrutinized despite new secured programs to authenticate legal voters with absolute credibility. This will become a US Supreme Court issue as political institutions jostle to prevent their sense of control. This may require the emergence of a third political party.

8. The federal government must consider a crisis protocol to allow elected officials the latitude of absentee votes by congressmen and senators in the face of situations similar to COVID-19.

9. Remote employment of some workforce should become a larger growth sector of the job market. Small businesses, especially, will look to this less expensive option. Part-time remote office specialty workers will emerge as a post-pandemic nuance.

10. The growth of online religious services will likely decimate in-person church attendance. A secondary impact on personal tithing could disrupt traditional financial support. Even traditional congregations and faiths must adapt to this growing segment of spirituality.

11. Every government entity from local to federal will develop protocols that include a list of essential and necessary workers and organizations. Likewise, the media must assist as part of the emergency management by dispensing timely and accurate information.

12. While it may be that investigative research will point to corrupt and irresponsible action/inaction taken by the Chinese government, safeguards of disease control must be elevated. The CoVID-19 pandemic will likely impair relationships between China and the US (and its allies) for decades. China's financial standing could be modified by demanded reparations they will contest.

Lastly, do not discount the demands of the masses. People will rise to be heard. Some of what is conceptualized above will lead into other spheres. People are affronted by a lackluster congress, especially in the face of dire need. The infighting and gridlock for a body that consistently grades less than ten percent for effectiveness in the public consciousness will trigger a reprisal. Beyond the idea of an emerging third party, there could likely be other landmark transitions in store. Term limitations have long been discussed. Some of the other privileges of office should be re-examined. Relationships with Political Action Committees (PACs), large donors with special interests, and the over-emphasis of corporate lobbyists will dissipate at the demand of the American voter.

Afterword

The world stopped. It was still on its axis and the synchronicity motions were intact, but the everyday activities were arrested with an undetermined and unscheduled return to normalcy. In varying degrees, world citizens were struck by what would follow—much by speculation, but mostly by the colossal impact of COVID-19's lessons of personal hygiene, social distancing, and abysmal economic adjustments.

It became apparent that many of the customs and traditions of humanity would, by this horrible spread of misery, need change. Those changes would impact travel, agriculture, market economies, human interaction, work sites, leisure, religion, entertainment, and other key elements of living everyday life.

Much of what could be coming hither would heretofore be unimagined. This book was done to explore what we know now but is left pondering what will be. What impositions will come about that alter constitutional rights or fundamental modes of living "in the pursuit of happiness?" What new authoritative federal or state agencies may be constituted in the aftermath of a dire and widespread public calamity? What will follow in job growth, medical advancements, or income opportunities. How long before we will feel safe again to travel, to stay in a hotel, to book a cruise? What will restaurants do differently? The aftermath will surely spawn many more questions than elicit answers.

History is a dark-hearted professor. The subject taught is "Mankind." The great experiment of individual liberty is less than 250 years old. We enjoy its sacrifice. Its example spurred other revolutions around the world.

Totalitarian regimes—history shows—all fail eventually. Read the list from serfdom, to Fascism, to Nazism. And yet there are those who attack capitalism—the entrepreneurial spirit that made America into the envy of others. Our industrial might is unmatched. Our innovations to benefit all world citizens are immense. It is capitalism that provides the shield for our freedoms.

Post pandemic geo-political issues will change.

Cause is the ultimate catalyst. Cause can encompass issues one opposes—or those that one supports. Causes are the issues that impact you, your community, and/or your lifestyle. It may be the cost-of-living, over-regulation, social agendas, education, a declining environment, or jobs. Pre-pandemic hot topics included tax reform, immigration, and foreign policy.

Our post pandemic cause is to sew us back together as one America! This as a dire and timely cause. But how?

Politics and politicians have, too often, gotten in the way. Most people, statistically, are NOT strictly party-affiliated. They are independent thinkers. We like those people the best! They are saying, "one size does not fit all." Constrained thinking breeds unproductive results. The total buy-in of those that blindly follow a candidate because of the 'D' or 'R' behind their name is ruinous to the country. Most Americans have crossed over and supported many Ds & Rs over time simply because they thought they were better people with more open ideas. The key is to know yourself first.

For instance, some tend to be more conservative on many issues, but not all. A lifetime conservative could still be open enough to comprehend a clear cause for protecting our natural environment. Some candidates decimate this cause. Another aspect that conservatives should re-evaluate is the consumption of marijuana—both as a medical and a recreational substance. Perhaps there is a growing sense that the illegal marijuana issue is hyped. People are still in jail for its abuse. Empirical evidence suggests that there is much less concern for a marijuana user than there would be for a social drinker. Drunk driving statistics bear this out. They are abysmal. Society will eventually arrive at universal conclusions that marijuana derivatives may be quite beneficial to cancer patients and the elderly. Besides, we're jailing the people who could be adding much to our state and federal tax revenues.

Our military is our ultimate defender of all liberties. We should cringe when we read about significant cutbacks in defense spending. Spending cutbacks have forced a weakening consequence that fosters dangerous vulnerability. There are those foreign regimes extant that want to erase America. Our military needs to be the most advanced and efficient in the world. It shields us from those that want to bring harm to our shores.

In general, the more we can educate ourselves to the issues, the more qualified we become as a voter/supporter of causes. Yet the vast majority of voters are blind. They take only seconds to post their preference to a straight D or R ticket. As we are often reminded, our first duty is to vote. Better said, our duty is to learn the candidates and the issues first, then vote. People with Ds and Rs are not always who you may think. As is often the case, these designations have a big tent. There are Libertarians, Socialists, Moderates, Liberals, and Tea Party-ites. By many estimates, only 15% of Americans know the candidates and/or the issues. The other 85% can be swayed by the massive marketing it takes to win an election. That's where the money matters. That is both an alarming and a sad statistic.

These last two decades have been a lesson in unbending party politics that have stifled every American in some way. The media, on both sides, is complicit. One could instantaneously change channels to encounter two completely opposite viewpoints describing the same incident or presidential comment. News programs do not report the news anymore. They report their jaded version of how the viewer should think.

The frequent federal gridlock and use of simple majority legislation have been detrimental to the common citizen. The post pandemic world has a chance to change the vitriolic behavior by raising their collective voices.

Timing is right for a third consequential party to move agendas forward. The third party will need to advocate a populist-centric position that can improve who we are and how we advance society. A third-party platform could embrace elements missing in the other two such as term limitations or a balanced federal budget. As discussed in an earlier chapter, and without too much more impetus, the states can call for a Constitutional Convention for that purpose. People can demand these things from their state governments.

In addition to federal term limits and a federal balanced budget amendment, a post-pandemic platform should consider a consumption tax, and a means to vote electronically for every legally authorized and verified citizen. There could be many other upgrades to a system that 71% of Americans feel is broken.[82]

Our original concept of sending a politician to Washington as a citizen-servant has turned into a monster. Senators are corporations. House members are full-time fundraisers who spend minimal time doing the work of the people. Lobbyists have become too important to them—more important than the people who placed them there. It's a horrible system. Term limits should be two terms for a senator—twelve years, and four terms for a congressman—8 years. It would force the "do nothing congress" to reach out across the aisle—a dinosaur of the past. A third party would guarantee cooperative results.

Most Americans would endorse a balanced budget (74%)[83], a major change in income taxes (88%)[84], and term limits (82%).[85] A third party could represent the will of the citizenry in these matters and explore other beneficial solutions for a greater America.

There have been other third parties. Ross Perot in 1992 received 19% of the presidential vote as the Reform Party. Teddy Roosevelt ran on the Bull Moose Party in 1912 and won eight states but lost to Woodrow Wilson (D).

The previous problems of initiating third parties to the American consciousness is that they start as "top-down" with a presidential candidate. A "bottom-up" third party would be more effective—by gaining momentum in local, statewide, and US house/senate elections. Eventually, a third party could elect a president.

Pat Caddell became a pioneer in political polling in high school!
Photo courtesy Breitbart News

The late Pat Caddell (1950-2019) felt strongly that a third party would fix many of the problems in Washington. Caddell worked on the Walter Mondale (D) campaign in 1972 and became famous as the Jimmy Carter (D) campaign strategist in 1976. He'd become known as a brilliantly wide thinker. As his career developed, he famously remarked that he "left the party of the corrupt only to be shunned by the party of the inept."[86] He became a third party of one, which he called the American Party.

Those that coddled his advice found him to be boldly frank. His accuracy of determining the heartbeat of the American voter may have been unparalleled.

> *"A politician's willingness to listen to good advice rises in inverse proportion to how badly he thinks he is doing."*[87]

His justification for a third political party was simple. He believed that the two choices had both become difficult selections for the American voter. He saw the rise of egos, special interests, corruption, and the general disingenuousness of many long-term legislators.

But starting a third party posed immense obstacles.

There was a time in American politics when it was relatively easy to jump-start a new political party and get it into the mainstream. That was how the Republican Party—the only third party in American history to become a major party—displaced the Whigs (along with several smaller parties) between 1854, when it was founded, and 1860, when it propelled Abraham Lincoln to the presidency.

It took three things to create a party back then: people, money, and ballots. Parties were responsible not only for recruiting and nominating candidates for office, but they also printed and distributed their own ballots (typically with the help of partisan newspaper publishers). Thus, there were very few barriers to entry: Candidates didn't have to petition to appear on a ballot, and new parties were free to endorse candidates from the more major parties, so their nominees ran less risk of being labeled spoilers. Essentially, parties could contest for power just as soon as they had backers and supporters... That's no longer possible: Today, third parties can't mount their own presidential bids after they learn whom the two major parties have nominated— there simply isn't enough time between the end of primary season and the general election to gain meaningful ballot access in enough states to win an Electoral College victory.[88]

The challenges are many.

The idea is to start the late Pat Caddell's American Party on school boards and city councils. The platforms for these candidates would come under the heading of "common sense reform." Once they begin electing state house members and state senators, they could advance their reforms to cement their legitimacy through governorships. The funding will follow, and the national movement would naturally sequence forward. People need a third choice because the greater need is for responsive and efficiently modern government. A third party could find the common ground that the other two established national parties have historically not considered. Most Americans are in that third column that advocates working together to achieve a better America.

In many other democratic countries, there are five or six parties. So, who would do everything possible to stop a third party? Answer: The other two.

Both major political "machines" would be compromised well into the future. Stay tuned. Much is about to change at "warp" speed.

Acknowledgements

The author acknowledges the expeditious work of the Palmetto Publishing Company, and its main promotional team of Jack Joseph, Erin Miller, and Abbey Suchoski. The sheer force of momentum moved this project from the optimism of two weeks to complete to the business transition of compression allowing four weeks to publish. It presented a record time of engagement that took an experienced and reactive team to accomplish.

Much appreciation is accorded to my brilliant friend, Frank Abagnale—a rare breed as a person of tremendous integrity, insight, and humility. Frank became a "go to" guy on matters of electronic security and its social implications.

Other appreciation is directed to two professors at the Harvard University graduate school in the political science program—George Wendt and John Paul Rollert. They have been kind enough to host me to lecture their students twice despite my sometimes-controversial insights on the two-party political system that, in my opinion, often stymies our great country.

Though my friend Pat Caddell passed away in early 2019, he remains high in my acknowledgement because of his unquestionable patriotism, enthused discourse, and careful construction of conventions he felt would benefit all mankind. He was a thinking man's thinker.

I would be remiss not thanking a late-life mentor, Major General James E. Livingston, USMC retired, a recipient of the Medal of Honor. Jim has lifted me in many ways, but mostly by his example of fortitude and perseverance.

Without family I would be missing so much that is meaningful in life. To my dear wife, Amanda, my children Billy, Joey, Katie, and Thomas—and the four grandchildren—I acknowledge and applaud your support. I also acknowledge my stepson, Austin Smith. My daughter, Katie McQueeney Altman, assisted me with edits even though she cannot spel guud enuff.

I was fortunate to be born into a struggling 1950s family with two outstanding parents and eight special siblings. We made it through because of each other. That early life experience was a golden epoch in every way with the exception of money.

Around the time that the COVID-19 coronavirus had begun to infect the Wuhan citizenry, I was encountering the first of two delicate brain surgeries at the Medical University of South Carolina. The second surgery was completed near the time of the Chinese travel ban (January 31). I just wanted to get out of the hospital! I returned a few day later because of complications. I had developed blood clots in my lungs which required yet another stay. The tests, hospitalizations and surgeries amounted to nearly $1 million in medical costs prompting me to point out two truths.

1. Medical costs are well out-of-line.
2. I *just ain't worth* that much.

The lingering effects in addition to a shortness of breath included my difficulty in swallowing solid foods and the loss of my voice. As I close this book, I still have trouble speaking. I called my second son in Denver the day before writing this Acknowledgement section. He could not understand much of what I said. I was more disappointed than he imagined, but I remembered those that could not speak at all, or could not see, or hear. There are many blessings to gather.

At every appointment throughout the ordeal I was asked if I was depressed. Depressed? Really? I had survived two difficult surgeries and woke up without my major concerns of loss—my full mental capacity, my memories, my optimism, and my God-given ability to laugh at myself. The weak and raspy vocal cords became the ticket price to be upright and happy. I have known well-too-many friends and family who were delivered the harshness of doomed prognoses. Whatever I would endure would be inconsequential to so many of those who I had deeply admired who have passed.

The surgeries were difficult, and at one time I thought I was not going to make it. That's when I accepted whatever fate emerged and thanked God for giving me so many blessings and an overabundance of caring friends. The experience also gave me some perspective for what I have written down in this production.

If there is a salient message to be taken from this work, I hope that it compels us as Americans to become proactive in re-uniting our country. The pandemic gave us time to settle in our minds what our lives should produce. We have a chance—all of us—to impart a positive human consequence past this tragic pause. Though the wellspring of my ideology has been mostly conservative, I have open ears to new principles and concepts. What I have noticed is that the extreme conservative shares space with the extreme liberal in one regard. These people have tongues but no ears. Conversely, middle America has the ability to adapt. In my own world, one would not have guessed that I advocate legalizing marijuana. My views on legalizing marijuana are pure. I've never taken an illegal drug, marijuana included. I have never even smoked a normal cigarette! But the medical and social empiricism combined with the economics win the day.

I strongly advocate a third political party to be formed from the grass roots of the people's mandate. That party would be charged with responsibilities to change the way we do things poorly into the best ways available by the technologies we have invented. By not accepting the repression of such by the media and the staid answers of the politicians, that third party will dictate the greatest future for our coming generations.

The coronavirus set the stage for our reinvestigation of ourselves. The millions of contractions delivered a death rate that averaged nearly 4% worldwide. Though it could have been much worse, these deaths will exceed 200,000 before this book is printed. There are a multiple of that number in the families who grieve the horrific and heartfelt losses. Let's reverently salute those families and pray for those lost to this preventable tragedy.

On Friday, April 17, the tenth and last day of this effort before the edits began, I received the sad news that Bennie Adkins died of the COVID-19 coronavirus. He had contracted it two weeks earlier. His daughter, Mary Ann, shared the difficult news. She could not visit him. I had met Bennie at several events. I enjoyed his outreach to others, especially his personal story of joining the Army as a foot soldier and earning a college degree and two master's degrees. He was a hero to his family. Indeed, Bennie was a humble hero to every American. A Vietnam War veteran, "during the 38-hour battle and 48-hours of escape and evasion, Adkins fought with mortars, machine guns, recoilless rifles, small arms, and hand grenades, killing an estimated 135-175 of the enemy and sustaining 18 different wounds,"[89] while saving the lives of others. He was a recipient of the Medal of Honor. May he rest in peace.

Command Sergeant Major Bennie G. Adkins Recipient, Medal of Honor

In time they will lay me away. But I hope they do not lay away the ideas and ideals that can be improved upon with heedful germination to make our country a better place for the generations that follow. The pandemic has become a part of who we are. We should all commit to a response from that adversity to becoming a force for something positive in honor of those who have perished.

About the Author

Author W. Thomas McQueeney

Author W. Thomas McQueeney has written a dozen books across genres to include history, biography, literary subjects, humor, and current events. He has written a novel, as well. As a humorist, he had authored over one hundred columns for the *Lowcountry Senior Sun*.

McQueeney has distinguished his career in other philanthropic and community venues to include chairmanship of The Congressional Medal of Honor Museum Foundation, Inc., The Citadel's Johnson Hagood Stadium Revitalization completion, and the Charleston Metro Sports Council. He served as president of the State of South Carolina Athletic Hall of Fame and on the board of directors of the National Council of Readiness and Preparedness, post 911. He served as a director of Bon Secours St. Francis Xavier Hospital, Our Lady of Mercy Community Outreach, and the Medical University of South Carolina Children's Hospital Development Board.

The author was elected by the State of South Carolina Legislature to serve on the Board of Visitors at The Citadel, his alma mater where he graduated in 1974 with a Bachelor of Arts degree in English. He also served on The Citadel Foundation Board for eight years. He is a recipient of several community and regional awards to include The Order of the Palmetto, the highest award accorded a citizen of the State of South Carolina.

He is married and has four children and four grandchildren.

Endnotes and References

1   The Praise of folly, 1509. https://study.com/academy/lesson/the-praise-of-folly-by-erasmus-summary-analysis-quiz.html

2   In Praise of Folly description. https://store.doverpublications.com/0486426890.html?gclid=Cj0KCQjw4dr0BRCxARIsAKUNjWRHB6nvPHVF7FyBOfFZAXF9BTcIYd3Jt3s1_iQMKHDFwWdDsbby4fkaAs3LEALw_wcB

3   Ode: Intimations of Immortality. William Wordsworth. https://www.bartleby.com/101/536.html

4   Worldwide Airline Traffic Daily. https://www.faa.gov/air_traffic/by_the_numbers/

5   Coronavirus name. https://directorsblog.nih.gov/2020/03/26/genomic-research-points-to-natural-origin-of-covid-19/

6   Pangolin. https://www.worldwildlife.org/stories/what-is-a-pangolin

7   Wuhan deaths. https://www.newsweek.com/wuhan-covid-19-death-toll-may-tens-thousands-data-cremations-shipments-urns-suggest-1494914

8   Urn orders. https://www.msn.com/en-us/news/world/wuhan-covid-19-deaths-may-be-in-tens-of-thousands-data-on-cremations-show/ar-BB11T0Vb

9   Authoritative regimes. http://img.gawkerassets.com/img/182h4jpdfjpaijpg/original.jpg

10 China Culpability. https://www.justsecurity.org/69398/chinas-responsibility-for-the-global-pandemic/

11 Wuhan. https://worldpopulationreview.com/world-cities/

12 Wet Markets. https://www.justsecurity.org/69398/chinas-responsibility-for-the-global-pandemic/

13 UCANews. https://www.ucanews.com/news/the-chinese-regime-and-its-moral-culpability-for-covid-19/87609

14 Spanish Flu. https://www.cdc.gov/flu/pandemic-resources/1918-commemoration/1918-pandemic-history.htm

15 Spanish Flu Deaths. https://www.nytimes.com/2012/04/03/science/civil-war-toll-up-by-20-percent-in-new-estimate.html

16 Black Death. https://www.history.com/topics/middle-ages/black-death

17 Bubonic Plague. https://www.mayoclinic.org/diseases-conditions/plague/symptoms-causes/syc-20351291

18 Plague of Justinian. https://www.mphonline.org/worst-pandemics-in-history/

19 Edward Jenner. https://www.historyofvaccines.org/timeline/all

20 Spread of Virus. https://www.worldometers.info/coronavirus/countries-where-coronavirus-has-spread/

21 Johnstown Times-Democrat. https://www.tribdem.com/coronavirus/governors-covid-19-stay-at-home-exemptions-listed/article_afab6c92-7436-11ea-97bf-83730c25991f.html

22 Easter Drive Through. https://www.the-sun.com/news/672892/mississippi-fined-500-praying-drive-in-church-service-easter-sunday/

23 Effectiveness of Quarantine. https://www.cebm.net/covid-19/is-a-14-day-quarantine-effective-against-the-spread-of-covid-19/

24 Declining Marriage Statistics. https://www.heritage.org/marriage-and-family/heritage-explains/why-the-declining-marriage-rate-affects-everyone

25 Declining Birth Rate. https://www.npr.org/2019/05/15/723518379/u-s-births-fell-to-a-32-year-low-in-2018-cdc-says-birthrate-is-at-record-level

26 Living alone. https://ourworldindata.org/living-alone

27 Congressional infections. https://www.cnn.com/2020/03/19/politics/coronavirus-test-positive-lawmakers-list/index.html

28 Frank Abagnale. https://www.govconwire.com/2020/04/well-known-security-expert-frank-abagnale-explains-why-irs-data-issues-hurt-cares-act/

29 Payroll Protection Program. https://thehill.com/policy/finance/492919-small-business-loan-program-runs-out-of-funds-amid-debate-over-new-bill

30 Estimate of illegal immigrants in US. https://www.brookings.edu/policy2020/votervital/how-many-undocumented-immigrants-are-in-the-united-states-and-who-are-they/

31 Center for Disease Control. https://www.cdc.gov/about/organization/mission.htm

32 Alcohol Sales Increase. https://www.marketwatch.com/story/us-alcohol-sales-spike-during-coronavirus-outbreak-2020-04-01

33 CARES Act. https://www.govconwire.com/2020/04/well-known-security-expert-frank-abagnale-explains-why-irs-data-issues-hurt-cares-act/

34 IBID.

35 IBID.

36 Carnival Cruise Lines. https://www.cruisemapper.com/wiki/758-cruise-ship-registry-flags-of-convenience-flag-state-control

37 IBID.

38 Airline Assistance Package. https://www.nytimes.com/2020/04/14/business/coronavirus-airlines-bailout-treasury-department.html

39 Single Households. https://www.statista.com/statistics/242284/percentage-of-single-person-households-in-the-us-by-state/

40 Comedy in the Face of Tragedy. https://www.nbcnews.com/think/opinion/snl-zoom-skits-coronavirus-rhapsody-benefits-limits-pandemic-parody-ncna1182966

41 Fan Attendance Decline. https://ugawire.usatoday.com/2019/03/27/college-football-game-attendance-still-on-the-decline-why-whats-the-solution-how-does-it-relate-to-uga-football/

42 Online College Growth. https://www.insidehighered.com/digital-learning/article/2019/12/17/colleges-and-universities-most-online-students-2018

43 IBID.

44 Pending BB Legislation. https://www.coloradofiscal.org/2019/02/a-constitutional-convention-is-closer-than-you-think/

45 Balanced Budget Amendment. https://www.pgpf.org/budget-basics/balanced-budget-amendment-pros-and-cons

46 IBID.

47 Jewish population. https://www.washington-post.com/news/post-nation/wp/2018/02/23/measuring-the-size-of-the-u-s-jewish-population-comes-down-to-identity/

48 Unchurched. https://www.patheos.com/blogs/geneveith/2017/06/churched-unchurched-dechurched-draft/

49 Lakewood Church. https://blog.capterra.com/the-5-biggest-online-churches/

50 Life Church. IBID.

51 Saddleback Church. IBID.

52 Church Statistical report. https://blog.capterra.com/church-statistics-social-media/

53 Catholic church attendance. https://news.gallup.com/poll/232226/church-atten-dance-among-catholics-resumes-downward-slide.aspx

54 Evangelical Growth. https://factsandtrends.net/2018/03/22/us-church-attendance-may-be-declining-but-not-among-evangelicals/

55 Millennial giving. https://www.patheos.com/blogs/geneveith/2020/02/the-coming-drop-off-in-church-giving/

56 Sub Sharan African mobile subscribers. https://www.zdnet.com/article/mobile-in-sub-saharan-africa-can-worlds-fastest-growing-mobile-region-keep-it-up/

57 Robotics. https://www.forbes.com/sites/shahinfarshchi/2020/04/10/expect-more-jobs-and-more-automation-in-the-post-covid-19-economy/#ff91b1929b40

58 Amazon. https://www.vox.com/recode/2020/4/10/21215953/amazon-fresh-walmart-grocery-delivery-coronavirus-retail-store-closures

59 Walmart. IBID.
60 Harvard Study. https://www.sciencealert.com/
    new-study-suggests-repeated-bouts-of-social-distancing-may-be-needed-until-2022
61 Market Drop Spanish flu. https://www.marketwatch.com/story/market-behavior-
    a-century-ago-suggests-the-worst-could-be-over-for-stocks-if-not-for-the-coronavi-
    rus-pandemic-2020-03-19
62 IBID.
63 Forbes article. https://www.forbes.com/sites/brianmenickella/2020/04/08/
    covid-19-worldwide-the-pandemics-impact-on-the-economy-and-
    markets/#51a42c5e28c3
64 Stay at Home Order. https://abcnews.go.com/Health/
    states-shut-essential-businesses-map/story?id=69770806
65 Bill Gates. https://mynorthwest.com/1791134/
    bill-gates-complete-shutdown-beat-coronavirus/?
66 Absentee Ballot Fraud. https://ballotpedia.org/Absentee_ballot_vote_fraud
67 Online Voting Concept. https://en.wikipedia.org/wiki/Voting
68 Voter Fraud. http://voterfraudfacts.com
69 College Basketball Revenue Loss. https://www.si.com/college/2020/03/26/
    ncaa-revenue-losses-march-madness-schools
70 NCAA losses. IBID.
71 Rudy Gobert. https://fivethirtyeight.com/features/
    the-coronaviruss-economic-effect-on-sports-could-be-staggering/
72 NBA Financial Losses. https://fivethirtyeight.com/features/
    the-coronaviruss-economic-effect-on-sports-could-be-staggering/
73 Masters Postponement. https://www.nytimes.com/2020/04/06/sports/golf/mas-
    ters-us-open-british-rescheduled.html
74 Loss of MLB revenue. http://source.southuniversity.edu/the-business-of-baseball-
    it-pays-to-host-spring-training-allstar-game-46512.aspx
75 Hollywood Reporter. https://www.hollywoodreporter.com/behind-screen/
    estimated-120000-iatse-jobs-lost-pandemic-1285229
76 New York Times on Hollywood impact. https://www.nytimes.com/apon-
    line/2020/03/31/us/ap-us-virus-outbreak-hollywood-impact.html
77 Russian outbreak. https://www.aljazeera.com/news/2020/04/coronavirus-deaths-
    slow-italy-france-live-updates-200413000419105.html
78 Russian COVID-19 cases. https://www.statista.com/statistics/1102303/
    coronavirus-new-cases-development-russia/
79 Owed to China. https://hbr.org/2020/02/
    how-much-money-does-the-world-owe-china
80 IBID.

81   IBID.

82   Broken System. https://www.commoncause.org/democracy-wire/
     most-americans-believe-system-broken/

83   Balanced Budget Poll. https://loudermilk.house.gov/uploadedfiles/bba_onepager_
     final.pdf

84   Major Change in Income Taxes. https://loudermilk.house.gov/uploadedfiles/
     bba_onepager_final.pdf

85   Term Limits. https://mclaughlinonline.com/2018/02/08/
     ma-poll-voters-overwhelmingly-support-term-limits-for-congress/

86   Pat Caddell. *The Rise of Charleston*, 2011.

87   Pat Caddell. https://www.azquotes.com/quote/1445721

88   Third Party Politics. https://newrepublic.com/article/146884/
     america-stuck-two-parties

89   Bennie Adkins Medal of Honor Citation. https://
     www.armytimes.com/news/your-army/2020/04/17/
     medal-of-honor-recipient-bennie-adkins-has-died-of-coronavirus/